Praise for Aligned Enchantment

"The book is absolutely beautiful! I completed Day 1, and it left me in happy tears...The journal feels so warm and safe. What a true treasure!" -Shawna Kiecker

"I got mine, and I teared up just reading and reflecting on Day 1. It's so beautiful I have to get over that and write in it!" -Stacey Christine

"I love Day 13 'Beloved' and dedication to Grandma! It brought tears of joy to my eyes - I love it so much. Rachel is a great storyteller, amazing painter/artist, and poet, and she reminds me so much of Grandma - she saw beauty in everything and could make a poem or song out of anything that she enjoyed. She is greatly missed." -Jeannette Ness

"I've been pondering so, so many things just since cracking it open a couple of days ago. So many heart-opening ways to explore and create meaningful alignment with my own sacred purpose." -Linda Forsyth (Wren)

"*Aligned Enchantment* is a beautiful journal with wonderful artwork and reflections!" -Betsy Anderson

"Rachel's exploration and growth have blossomed into a gentle, beautiful vehicle for us all to align and feel the enchantment of the tiny and huge moments in our own lives. What a gift." -Melanie Goldish

"I highly recommend this journal for all people, especially those who want to live a more joyful and enchanted life. I found Rachel's soulful poems, meditations, and stories soothing and engaging. I have read it cover to cover, and I cannot wait to begin using it and putting pen to paper. It is so beautiful, though, that I am not sure I can mark it up! Kudos to Rachel for sharing her heart with us." -Stacy Crawford

"My copy arrived today. I am amazed! Artwork and poetry are woven with prompts that spark writing. Rachel created a journal that feeds my soul." -Barb Perushek

"Rachel Gilbertson's *Aligned Enchantment* is full of beautiful illustrations with thought-provoking reflection questions. I enjoyed how each page offers the opportunity for self-discovery and inspiration." -Julie Zaruba Fountaine

"Rachel Gilbertson weaves beautiful illustrations with poignant reflection questions in *Aligned Enchantment*. Her experience as a health coach shines through as she provides daily thought-provoking inspiration. The book provides opportunities for readers to take pause and explore deeper connections with the surrounding world. Each page is like taking an enriching, meditative breath. The daily questions encourage readers to explore meaningful issues and include space for written reflections. Whether you are experiencing a life change or just looking for inspiration, this journal will help guide you to the answers you have within. I have journaled throughout the majority of my life. This is one journal I will most definitely treasure". -Kerry K. Fierke

Aligned Enchantment in the Classroom

As a busy Mom of 3 active children, high school educator, daughter, and friend, I am constantly on the go! Although I practiced meditation years ago, I had unintentionally let those moments of quiet reflection and finding my inner peace escape me in the struggle of the juggle of the day-to-day chaos.

When I ordered *Aligned Enchantment,* I was not sure what to expect. Would I need to commit and find more time that I already did not have in my day to sit under a tree somewhere in silence when I can't seem to even be able to sneak away to use the restroom without someone needing me?

So I decided to implement it as a way to support Social and Emotional Learning in my high school classroom in one of my elective classes. After Day 1, I was hooked!

Not only is this book extremely easy to read and comprehend, it is easy to navigate. The daily exercises are short and range from 5 to 15 minutes, perfect for my schedule in and out of the classroom! The best part is that these self-reflections and meditations can be done anywhere and with anyone!

Over the last few weeks, I have found myself revisiting these daily practices while waiting for my kids to finish their activities in my classroom and even sharing with co-workers out of pure excitement and joy of my personal self-discovery!

If you are new to self-reflection and meditation and want an easy-to-follow and time-friendly practice, you can do anytime, anywhere to help rediscover your inner peace and emotions and help you feel more grounded in your daily 'struggle of the juggle,' this is the book for you!

- Jolene, Menahga High School Student Success Coordinator

Student Reflections

"I started this book last month in one of my elective classes. It is an amazing meditation book that truly helped me reflect and bloom at a transitional time in my life with High School Graduation just around the corner. It beautifully guides you to explore your inner self, embrace mindfulness, and discover a sense of peace and growth. The author's insightful wisdom and practical exercises make it a transformative journey that is inspiring and brings me daily joy. I highly recommend this book for anyone seeking inner clarity and personal growth!"

12th Grade Student

"Great techniques for all ages! This book contains great strategies for mindfulness and self-reflection. It has helped prompt me to reconnect with my inner child and rediscover those simple acts of joy that surround me in my daily life. I love how the author breaks down the daily word into the various ways it can be used, incorporated, and understood. I highly recommend this book for self-growth as well as for those who enjoy participating in meditation and self-reflection as a group or with friends!"

10th Grade Student

"I recently started this incredible meditation book in one of my elective classes. It has truly brought so much clarity and helped me in healing my inner child. It gently guides you through practices that uncover deep-rooted emotions, allowing for healing and growth. It's a powerful tool for reconnecting with your true self and finding inner peace. Highly recommend it for anyone seeking clarity and inner healing!"

10th Grade Student

Aligned Enchantment

Rachel Gilbertson M.Ed., NBC-HWC

REL Print Group, a Hezzie Mae publication
Duluth, MN.
www.HezzieMae.com

ISBN: 979-8-9886309-7-5

Interior Design: Heather N. Wilde, HezzieMae.com

Dedication

This journal is dedicated to my late Grandma Frances,
whose presence continued to show up throughout this project.

She lived her life wholeheartedly.

She danced with us grandkids around the kitchen while
singing her famous little diddy.
She penned her poems about the raindrops and the robins.
She made up songs and sang them to the cows.

She generously shared her grace and compassion.
She embodied unconditional love.

*"Live each day as though it
may be the last.
Fill it with richness of charity and
love for others and happiness will
be yours."*
-Grandma Frances

Disclaimers

The selection of words, definitions, and etymology presented here was approached through a creative lens rather than a strictly grammatical one. We encourage you to read and appreciate the creative energy with which they are presented. Sources are listed in the Bibliography.

Aligned Enchantment is a journal designed to support self-reflection. It includes reflective questions that may evoke difficult memories and strong emotions. Individuals with trauma or mental health concerns are encouraged to seek support from a professional counselor while using this journal as needed.

Dear Reader,

Words cannot fully express how delighted I am for you to be holding this journal in your hands.

Thank you for supporting my dreams of being an artist and author. I am grateful you have accepted this invitation to embark on a 100-day journey of inspiration and insight. Before we jump in, I'd love to share a little story of how this came to be.

Once upon a time in the summer of 2023, I participated in Sarah Seidelmann's Creative Soul Retrieval group, where I and 35 others committed to creating something every day for at least 84 days (with the option to extend to 100 days). Each of us picked individual projects that entailed doing something that brought joy and enchantment (i.e., coloring, painting, writing, singing, photography, landscaping, or anything else we wanted to do).

The guidance was to pick something we could do in about 15 minutes each day. It could be more or less, but the idea was to simply create daily and see what happened.

I embarked on an adventure of being open to enchantment and following inspiration by creating a mini watercolor painting each day for 100 days. I wanted to learn more about watercolor painting; I love words and their meanings, and I find the practice of reflection to be powerful. Therefore, I braided these elements together and called it "Aligned Enchantment." Each day, an image would catch my eye, or a word would resonate, and it would become the day's theme, which I then paired with reflective questions.

The Creative Soul Retrieval group participants posted daily in a private Facebook group and refrained from commenting on each other's creations. It wasn't about likes or feedback, only the process. Sharing outside of the group was optional, for instance, posting on our own personal social media.

I also decided to share my daily creations and reflections on my Art of Presence social media pages. Although I noticed thoughts of comparison and 'not good enough' related to this project along the way, I also felt a growing sense of confidence as the days passed.

The commitment to painting and posting daily helped to loosen the knots of expectation and perfection. I got to a point of "good enough," posted it, and then let it go. I was focused on the intention that this process didn't need to result in anything.

I had no idea this would eventually be published as a journal. Honestly, I know it would have changed the project if I had added that layer of exposure and potential pressure at the start.

Some days, my project flowed quickly and easily; other days, inspiration was more elusive, and it felt like a stretch to pull it all together. Sometimes, the word would come first. Other times, the image became crystal clear, or a question would surface for me to ponder.

These clues would emerge over the day, even though I initially planned to complete my project in the morning. The painting usually took around 15 minutes, but the reflections and posting took longer.

As much as I wanted to confine this project into a set time and space, inspiration wanted more freedom, and enchantment refused to be rushed.

Along the way, I worried I had taken on more than I could handle as I struggled to fit it in and fell behind in posting daily. Of course, the Creative Soul Retrieval group was a non-judgmental space, and we each had the artistic freedom to change our minds or projects at any time.

About every ten days, I noticed the urge to switch gears and change the theme by dropping the word, black box outline, or reflection component. There were days that the words wouldn't come to me on my timeline, or when they did, I wondered if they distracted me from the image.

At times, the lined borders felt limiting, and I worried I confined my creativity within those black squares. The black accents seemed to swing between not enough and too much.

However, each time I sat with these thoughts long enough, a whisper of a word or inkling of an image would encourage me to stick with it.

Curiosity invited me to wonder what the collective result would be as I continued to add to this over the summer. So I carried on.

Of course, now I am especially grateful for these insights and the parameters I've set with size, shape, and overall similarity of style between my mini paintings so they could end up in this journal.

Although I initially thought I'd paint in the mornings, I intentionally picked a portable project as I knew my days would be full of work and family functions. Many days, my mini watercolors were painted in the evening in the dance studio lobby, outside at baseball practice, or while waiting in the car.

Only in reflecting on this process could I see that the mini painting was also a message to focus on the small moments.

Looking back, I can see the themes and lessons this project taught me.

- *Follow intuition and sparks of inspiration.*
- *Trust the unfolding and let go of a specific outcome*
- *Try new things and make space for messes and mistakes. Sometimes, a 'mistake' turns out better than you imagine ('Happy little accidents," as Bob Ross would say)*
- *Play, exercise imagination, and practice perspective-taking*
- *Hone in on what resonates. Images, colors, and words begin to stand out when you're paying attention.*
- *Observe thoughts and behaviors around creativity and tangibly work with fears and tired storylines: Who am I to do this? Am I good enough? Do I have permission to do this?*
- *Practice vulnerability by sharing something that feels so personal yet is universal.*

My greatest hope for this journal is that it allows your inner wisdom to emerge. I hope you notice any inklings of insights arise, you feel any glimpses of soul shimmers, and that you follow the subtle hints of curiosity.

I have found that intuition, enchantment, and inspiration hang out in these seemingly insignificant places. The extraordinary is hidden in the ordinary, not just grand gestures or big, bold moves.

It is in your hands now because you are the reader and author of this story. I can't wait to see what unfolds.

With Love,

Let the Journey Begin...

Rachel
Headstart 1988

2017

treasured - treasuring - treasures

1. to keep or regard as **precious; value highly**.
2. synonym: **appreciate**
3. to accumulate and store away, as for future use

origin

The English word treasure comes from
the Old French tresor, both meaning
"**something of great worth**"

Day 1: Treasure

Today's inspiration is "treasure." I found this antique mop bucket on our family farm several years ago and revitalized it for some sentimental, shabby chic decor. A treasured piece of history.

Reflection Questions

Who and what do you treasure?

How might you see the treasure in something ordinary today?

What helps your inner child feel treasured, precious, and appreciated?

bloom

blooming - blooms - bloomed

1. to bear a **flower** or flowers
2. to support plant life with **abundance**
3. to **glow**, be **radiant**
4. to mature or **flourish** with youth and vigor
5. to appear to **come into being** suddenly

origin

Latin: *flos* "**flower**"
florere "to **blossom, flourish**"
extended form of root bhel "**to thrive, bloom**"

Day 2: Bloom

This beautiful tree in our yard is in bloom for approximately one week each spring.
It's a time to notice and savor its radiance.

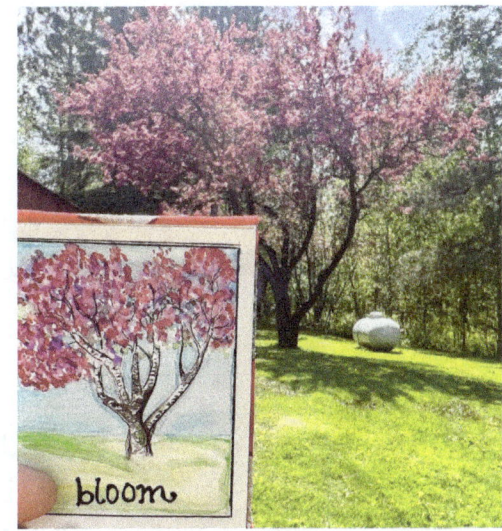

Reflection Questions

What do you notice is in bloom in your life?

How might you invite abundance and radiance into your day?

What parts of yourself have emerged, bloomed, and flourished over your lifetime?

whim - whimsical - whimsies

1. a capricious humor, **playful expression**
2. an odd or **fanciful notion**
3. anything playful or fanciful; as an **artistic creation**

origin

1640s "play on words, pun," shortened from **whimwham** "fanciful object" (q.v.)
Meaning "caprice, fancy, sudden turn or inclination of the mind" was first recorded in the 1690s, probably a shortened form of **whimsy.**

Day 3: Whimsy

I find this sweet little incense burner to be so whimsical. It was gifted to us by an aunt who visited Germany as a neat memento from her travels.

It also has been a portal of inspiration. Several months ago, one of my daughters sketched it, which inspired me to paint it and my son to paint it, too! You never know what might set off a chain reaction of inspiration.

Reflection Questions

What do you find whimsical?

How might you invite playful expression or a fanciful notion into your day?

Recall something that made you feel carefree as a kid, then do it again on a whim!... I highly recommend frolicking with your friends!

delightful - delighting - delighted

1. a high degree of **pleasure or enjoyment**; joy; rapture
2. to have or take great pleasure

origin
From Latin *delactare:*
"to allure, delight, charm, please"

Day 4: *Delight*

Sharing this feels a bit vulnerable because I worry you'll all think I'm silly, woo-woo, and/or weird.

However, if you've met me, that ship has probably already sailed. What's wrong with being silly, woo-woo, and weird anyway?!?

I also think it's important to destigmatize helpful practices that are considered woo-woo, so here it goes:

In preparation for this Creative Soul Retrieval project, participants were invited to free-write a letter from Enchantment to see what it would love to do.

Reflection Questions

Take a few minutes and free-write a letter from Enchantment. Could you just let the words flow without editing them?

How might you invite joy and pleasure into your day?

What brings delight to your inner child?

Dear Rachel,

Get in touch with magic, follow your intuition, and find delight, joy, and more of me, Enchantment. Follow the twinkles and shimmers of deeper knowing.

Trust the unfolding.

Have fun and play. It doesn't need to make sense or be for any other purpose other than pleasure.

Love, Enchantment

emerge

emerging - emerges- emerged

1. to **move out or away** from a surrounding fluid, covering, or shelter.
2. to come into view, to become conscious, to become known after being in obscurity.
3. to come into **existence**

origin

From Latin *emergere* "**bring forth**, bring to **light**," "**rise/arise** out or up, come forth, up, or out" from assimilated form of ex "**out**" + *mergere* "to **dip, sink**"

Reflection Questions

Day 5: *Emerge*

What is emerging in your life? What wants to break through?

Reflect on the phrase "I can hardly contain myself" and consider refusing to contain yourself when something exciting happens. What would that look and feel like?

Let your inner child take up space. What emerges?

I thought it would be fun to paint a mini watercolor version of my "Caterflies and Butterpillars" piece.

It's fun to see how inspiration emerges and evolves over time.

"Caterflies & Butterpillars: A Tethered Emerging of Transformation"

Do you ever imagine what it might be like for a claustrophobic caterpillar to find the courage to become a Badass & Brave butterfly? What arises when life turns upside down, tethered by a silky thread?

Might you relate to the worry of being wrapped up in intense emotions, fearing being consumed by them? But have you curiously considered that being cocooned in discomfort and breathing into constriction is the catalyst of transformation?

A chrysalis of compassion to fall apart and come together.

Easing anxiety
Tending tension
Holding hurt
Nurturing numbness
Soothing sorrow

In the midst of the messy middle of metamorphosis. The quiet quaking, shaking and shimmering from the inside out. Integrating the wisdom of the past, invitation of the present, and potential of the future.

Remembering ethereal nature is encapsulated in its essence.

Recollection. Reclamation. Revolution.

Have you experienced tension at the threshold of transition? Can you imagine how uncomfortable the pressure feels before the butterfly breaks through? Do you wonder if it grieves losing its grounded caterpillarness or surrendering its snug stuckness?

Contemplating what's on the other side as it holds its breath, contorts, and conforms to fit within its confines. Realizing that the tightness is an opportunity for release and expansion.

Relaxing the gripping, grasping, clenching, and clinging. Deciding not to be condensed or contained. Loosening the knots of external expectation and turning towards an internal guiding force of freedom. Finally, exhaling and emptying to create space. Slowly inhaling and filling up with inspiration.

Unfurling. Unfolding. Unshielded.

Dipping below the surface into a sacred space of deeper insight and trust. Through the breakdown and breakthrough into being beyond bounds.

Rupture. Relief. Reveal.

Spreading strong wings that flutter freely, bolstering bravery with each beat. Gliding into an adventure of exploration of the same wild and wonderous world but from a new perspective.

Glistening from the submerging, merging, and emerging. Aligned with inherent integrity, intuition, worthiness, and wholeness.

Embodied, Emboldened. Expanded.

trust

trusts - trusting - trusted

1. to have or place **confidence** in; **depend** on
2. to expect with **assurance**; assume
3. to give credence to, **believe**
4. to place in the **care** of another person or in a situation deemed safe; **entrust**

origin

c. 1200, from Old Norse *treysta*
"to trust, **rely** on, make **strong** and **safe**"

Day 6: Trust

As a health coach, I've had the honor of walking alongside many humans on their wellbeing paths. I'm grateful for them trusting me with their stories as they reflect on what is important to them while they work toward their goals. I support them in aligning intention, attention, attitude, action, and impact. One step at a time.

Habits are created by identifying values and beliefs, becoming aware of thoughts and emotions, consistently practicing goal-aligned behaviors, navigating challenges, and celebrating successes. This applies to wellbeing as well as any other facet of life. It requires both building trust and trusting the process.

Around this time last year, I noticed I wasn't trusting myself. I heard myself telling various people that although I had started this business, I didn't really know what I was doing. This limiting belief wasn't true.

I do know what I'm doing. I know the intentions I have, the direction I'm heading, and I see the next step. That's all, and that's enough. I don't have the whole journey mapped out in a sequence of strategic moves over multiple years. However, I also trust my intuition, inspiration, and serendipity. They show me the way, and I consistently show up. It doesn't feel like work in this way of being. It also relieves the stress of thinking there is only one right way to do something, as art often turns out better when things don't go as planned or expected.

I took this picture on a hike with my family last summer as I noticed everyone navigated through a portion of rocky terrain in their own way. It reminded me that even though we all were headed in the same direction, we took our own paths. Some bounded agility, while others proceeded with caution. I didn't plan out my steps in sequential order, but when I took one step, the next step appeared.

That's the way I feel about starting Art of Presence and all goals and decisions - big and small.
One step at a time.
One day at a time.

Trust *Reflection Questions*

What next step do you see in front of you right now?

What practices help you trust the process?

How can you let the parts of yourself that are worried or scared know that you can trust yourself to care of yourself?

Remind yourself that you are fully capable, creative, and complete, just as you are.

Certified Intrinsic Coach Training

frolic

frolicking - frolicked

1. to amuse oneself, **make merry**
2. to play and run about **happily, romp**

origin

From Middle Dutch *vrolyc* "happy," a compound of
vro- "**merry, glad**" + *lyc* "**like**"
Similar to 1811, *rollick*:
"be **jovial** in behavior," "moving in a careless,
swaggering manner; with a **frolicsome** air"

Day 7:  Frolic

I saw the tiniest fawn the other day, and it was delightful.
It frolicked off before I could get
a picture, but it inspired today's painting.

Reflection Questions

How might you amuse yourself today?

Move about in a careless, swaggering manner with a frolicsome air. What do you notice?

What did you love to play as a child? Could you try it and see if it still brings merriment?

unfurls - unfurling - unfurled

1. to **unroll, unfold**, or **spread out**
2. to be unrolled, unfolded, or **spread out from a furled state**

origin

1640s, from <u>un-</u> "opposite of" + <u>furl</u>
Furl from Latin *firmus*
*dher- "to hold firmly, support" + -lier "to bind"

Reflection Questions

What tension can you unfurl in your body or unwind in your mind?

What is growing and expanding in your life?

Go frolic near the ferns. What do you notice?

Day 8: Unfurl

Meditation by Rachel Gilbertson

This is an invitation from the ferns to pause and breathe...
Exhale...
Unroll your shoulders
Unclench your jaw
Uncurl your fists
Inhale...
Untighten your tummy
Unravel your nerves
Unfetter your frets
Exhale...
Holding your breath will not hold it all together
Inhale...
Fill up with inspiration and know it won't all fall apart when letting it go.
It's a release and an unfurling
Exhale...
Expel the air from your depths, dig into your desire
Inhale...
Expand in your width, grow into your wisdom
Exhale...
Extend into your full length, stretch toward your longing
Inhale...
Take up space
Repeat

changes - changing - changed

1. to become **different** or undergo **alteration**
2. to undergo **transformation** or **transition**
3. to go from one **phase** to another, as the moon or seasons

origin

from Old French *changier*
"to **change, alter; exchange, switch**,"

Day 9: *Change*

Change is upon us.

The arrival of summer break for the kids means that routines are in transition.

Holding on to helpful habits and timetables while also inviting ease and efficiency.

In the messy middle of a transition, piles of school paperwork and supplies manifest.

Craving clearing and creating space to see what comes as the season changes.

Today, I learned that "in almost every part of the world, the Dragonfly symbolizes change, transformation, adaptability, and self-realization.

The change often referred to has its source in mental and emotional maturity and understanding the deeper meaning of life." (Emily Fredericks Foundation, 2024).

Reflection Questions

What transitions are happening in your life, big or small?

How might you invite ease into changes that arise today?

Have you noticed how you've grown and changed, yet your essence remains unchanged?

Learn more about dragonfly symbolism from www.mindbodygreen.com

22

clarity

rMg

clear- clearing - cleared

1. the **clearness** of appearance
2. clearness of thought or style, **lucidity**

origin

from Latin *claritas*
"brightness, splendor,"

Day 10:  Clarity

Reflection Questions

Could you clarify what you need in your life right now?

How might you create space in your day?

Check out Al Jeffery's Meditation "Create a Clearing to Listen In" on the Insight Timer App. https://insig.ht/wYyqon0w9sb. What does it bring up for you?

> **"Clearing"**
> by Martha Postlethwaite
>
> Do not try to save
> the whole world
> or do anything grandiose.
> Instead, create
> a clearing
> in the dense forest
> of your life
> and wait there
> patiently,
> until the song
> that is your life
> falls into your own cupped
> hands
> and you recognize and greet
> it.
> Only then will you know
> how to give yourself to this
> world
> so worthy of rescue.

hope

hopes - hoping - hoped

1. to **wish** for a particular event that one considers possible
2. to have **confidence, trust**
3. to **desire** and consider **possible**

origin

From early 13c. as
"to wish for" (something), **"desire."**

Day 11: *Hope*

Today, I had the privilege of riding the first half of a 150-mile bike ride to raise awareness and money for the Multiple Sclerosis Society.

Today, I have hope.
I have hope for a lot of things.
I have hope that there will continue to be medical advancements.

In the last two decades, treatment options have greatly improved to help those diagnosed with MS live their best lives.

My family has directly benefited from medication advancements, and I'm grateful they've maintained my husband's health. I have hope that there will be a cure for MS.

Thanks to the generosity of many, groundbreaking research is being done to get closer to a cure. We are biking for a cure.

I have hope in humanity.

An event like the MS150 brings together people from all walks of life, ages, shapes, sizes, and ability levels. Although we are all uniquely different, we are all connected with a common sense of purpose.

The collective care and camaraderie of this event are special. I serendipitously met some lovely humans today that I hope to stay connected with.

I have hope.
I hope you have hope, too.
Because hope is contagious.

To donate to the MS Society
www.nationalmssociety.org/

Hope *Reflection Questions*

What do you have hope for? How are you actively working to create the change you want to see?

How might you invite possibility into today?

What did you wish for as a child?

"We are learning to listen to the intelligence of our hearts and act on that wisdom."

- Danielle Laporte

effervesce - effervescing

1. the property of forming bubbles: the action or process of **effervescing**
2. an appealing, **lively** quality; **high spirits** or **animation**

origin

Figurative sense of "**liveliness**" is from 1748

Day 12: *Effervescence*

Today, I completed the second half of the MS 150 and couldn't quite put the words to the collective energy of participating in a shared event with such hope, joy, purpose, and challenge.

I've participated in this and other fitness events where that camaraderie and energy are palpable, but I never had a word for it. So I googled it and learned that there is a name for this: **Collective Effervescence,** a term coined by French sociologist Emile Durkheim more than 100 years ago.

"Collective effervescence is the feeling of energy and harmony when people are engaged in a shared purpose. A joie de vivre (exuberant enjoyment of life) manifests when we share moments with others, such as being in a stadium that erupts in simultaneous applause when a musician returns for an encore performance" (Cohen, 2021).

Not only is the MS 150 an opportunity for collective effervescence, but it is also a tangible way to practice collective care. In a culture that values self-care but rarely talks about collective care, this event highlights that we all need each other.

From the volunteers that go the extra mile to put on this event, to the bikers including and encouraging each other along the way, from supporters cheering and ringing cowbells, to family and friends donating their hard-earned money to support an organization that helps those living with MS live their best lives. We are all in this together and need each other.

I'm grateful for the opportunity to experience collective effervescence for a great cause as we work towards practicing wellbeing for ourselves and supporting the wellbeing of each other.

Effervesence

Reflection Questions

When have you experienced collective effervescence?

How might you invite joy to bubble up today?

Go outside and blow some bubbles, just for fun! Invite others to join you.

"Connection is the energy that exists between people when they feel seen, heard, and valued; When they give and receive without judgment; And when they derive sustenance and strength from the relationship."

-Brené Brown

beloved

rMg

be loved - be love

1. **greatly loved, dear to the heart.**
2. a person who is **beloved, dearly loved**

origin

is attested from 1520s from
be- + loven "**to love**"
The noun meaning **"one who is beloved."**

Day 13: Beloved

I saw the sweetest robin the other day on my bike ride, and it reminded me of my Grandma Frances. I immediately could hear the song she made up that started with,

♪ "Robin dear, I love you so…" ♫

There were more verses, but I can't recall them. But I can still hear her sweet song. She was always singing, making up her own tunes. She sang to the birds in her yard, she sang to the cows on the farm, and she sang while she danced with us grandkids in her yellow-clad kitchen with her little diddy

♫ "A chunk a lunk lunk and a chunk a lunk lunk." ♪

Grandma Frances always had a smile on her face, a song to sing, and she never had a bad thing to say about anyone. She had a way of genuinely making each person feel seen and special. I'm pretty sure every one of us grandkids thought we were her favorite. She modeled compassion, care, and unconditional love. She is deeply missed by many.

I think of her often and still feel her presence. Along with making up her own songs, she also wrote lovely poetry. I like to imagine that when I get creative insights where words begin to flow, perhaps she's whispering them in my ear. I also believe Robin is a messenger of her reminder to love deeply.

Beloved is to Be Loved and to Be Love.
She is beloved.

Beloved *Reflection Questions*

Who is beloved to you?

How might you "Be Love(d)" today?

Who made you feel seen and special as a child?

"The most precious gift we can offer anyone is our attention. When mindfulness embraces those we love, They will bloom like flowers."

- Thich Nhat Hahn

care

cares - caring - cared

1. suffering of mind, **grief**
2. a disquieted state of mixed **uncertainty, apprehension**, and **responsibility**; a cause for **anxiety**
3. painstaking or watchful **attention**
4. **regard** coming from desire or esteem
5. charge or **supervision; responsibility** for or attention to health, well-being, and safety

origin

Old English *caru, cearu*
"**sorrow, anxiety, grief,**" also
"**burdens of mind**; serious mental attention, "

Day 14: Care

This is a little snapshot of part of my "Eternal Connection" piece. The word that came to mind was "care."

When I started putting this together, I was surprised to see these definitions pop up. But then, I realized I was thinking of soft, compassionate care.

However, to care is to take on responsibility, feel the weight of worry for another, and notice your attention is often on apprehension and anxiety for their wellbeing.

To care is hard work. Perhaps that's why some people push it down and pretend not to care.

"This is hard work and heart work," as Dr. Diane Banigo would say.

We use "caregivers" and "caretakers" interchangeably, but aren't they different: giving and taking? By definition, they can't always be reciprocal, so does resentment naturally bubble up with the endless to-dos between moments of great joy that are so unbearable to feel fully?

Is it hard to feel joy because we fear the grief would consume us if we were to suffer the loss? To care is to love, and the residue of love is grief.

In all this, the giving and the weight of responsibility are heavy. Could I ask for help? "*No thanks, I got this,*" says my current self as my inner 3-year-old yells. "*I can do it myself!*" I realize her independent refrain has been my anthem all along.

Lately, the phrase "*I trust myself to take care of myself*" has been a mantra of self-care; I also trust myself to take care of Us. Even though I believe in the goodness of humanity, I sometimes wonder if I trust Us to take care of ALL of Us. There are times when it seems some couldn't care less while others couldn't care more. The truth is that we need each other in a flow of give and take.

Give good care,
Take good care.

38

Care Reflection Questions

How do you care for your heart in the midst of this hard work?

What is one thing you can ask for help with today?

Practice fully feeling joy like you did as a child. Jot down what you notice.

Eternal Connection Reflection

This painting I made represents the everlasting love
between a caregiver and child.

Reflection co-created by Rachel Gilbertson and Tiara Cash
This painting also represents (start at the bottom)

How we heal ourselves along the way
An alignment
A befriending
A becoming
Belonging

How we sit with our precious self
tuned into the sacred space that creates
a clearing for purpose, peace, and possibility
Wrapped in protection
Reminded of our perseverance

How we care for ourselves
Swaddled in love
Cradled in compassion
Rocked and reassured of our worthiness

How we nurture our inner child,
are nourished by inspiration,
and are transformed by trusting our intuition
Grounded in gratitude for the gift of life itself
All moments, each heartbeat, every breath

shine

shined - shining

1. to emit **rays of light**
2. to be **bright** by **reflection** of light
3. to be **eminent, conspicuous, or distinguished**;
   to **perform** extremely well

origin

From Old English *scinan*
**"shed, send forth, or give out light;
be radiant, be resplendent, illuminate"**

Day 15: *Shine*

"The Solar Plexus Chakra empowers you to radiate your creative light out into the world. It gives you the confidence to shine!

Working on the third chakra is empowering. The sort of power we refer to is not 'power over.' Rather, it is the power to locate the sun at your center and shine that light into the world. In this way, you will become a beacon and light the way for others."
Jilly Shipway, *Chakras for Creativity*

This chakra is located at your center/core. It is associated with yellow and helps you radiate light out into the world with a sunny, optimistic outlook. I think of this as being "Soul-ar Powered."

It feels like goosebumps or tingles when something deeply resonates with you. I call these "Soul Shimmers" an embodied experience of your essence. It is also fiery like the sun and can help us access courage and channel anger into creating change. When there are struggles, I think about finding creative "Soul-utions" aligned with integrity.

Shine *Reflection Questions*

What helps you access your "Soul-ar Power"?

Think of something you're struggling with. Sit with it and see if creative "Soul-ultions" emerge from the stillness and silence.

Do something that lets your inner child shine! Grab crayons and doodle!

43

"We need writers, painters, and other creative visionaries to illuminate a fresh view of the world and inspire us all to work for change."

- Jilly Shipway, *Chakras for Creativity*

Kindness rMg

kind

1. the quality or state of being **kind**:
2. treating people with kindness and
respect: a kind deed; favor

Loving-kindness

May you be **safe**
May you be **happy**
May you be **healthy**
May you **live with ease**

Day 16: Kindness

I planted these succulents a while ago and admired their shape and color. I learned that succulents are known for their ability to hold water and persist through drought and difficulty.

Plants are great reminders to notice what seeds we're planting in our lives. A valuable practice I've found is to plant seeds of love and kindness through Metta Meditation, also known as Loving-kindness.

In mindfulness, there are many anchor points you can focus your attention on. Sometimes it's the breath, body sensations, sounds or saying mantras silently to yourself. In loving-kindness practice, your attention is focused on sending well-wishes to yourself and others.

Traditional phrases may be used, such as:
May I/you be safe
May I/you be happy
May I/you be healthy
May I/you live with ease

However, positive phrases can be used, and the practice can be done in several ways.

1. It generally starts with offering these phrases to yourself. This might feel tricky at first, but it can help to imagine yourself as you were as a young child.
2. Next, you bring a beloved person to mind and offer them loving-kindness. This can be anyone you love, admire, or are inspired by.
3. Then, you bring a neutral person to mind. This is an acquaintance or someone you interact with but don't know well, for instance, a grocery store clerk or bank teller. You extend the phrases of compassion and well-wishes to them.
4. The practice continues by offering loving-kindness to someone you find challenging. This doesn't have to be the person you find to be the most difficult. This can be tough, but it can also help to imagine them as a young child.
5. Finally, you expand your awareness to all creatures and beings everywhere, wishing we may all be safe, happy, healthy, and live with ease.

You can also practice what I like to call "Metta on the Move," where you simply and silently offer these well-wishes to strangers you encounter while you go about your day.

As Sharon Salzberg says, *"Loving-kindness meditation is a practice that can help dissolve the rigid labels of us vs. them. There is only us. It requires a willingness to stretch our attention and cultivate curiosity around our habitual ways of looking at ourselves and others...As you continue with loving-kindness practice, you may find that it transforms you in ways you weren't expecting."*

Reflection Questions

Offer loving-kindness to yourself as a child and then to yourself as you are now. What do you notice?

Offer loving-kindness to someone you hold dear or admire. What do you notice?

Offer loving-kindness to a neutral person and then to someone you struggle with. What do you notice?

Loving Kindness Practice

May you be safe
May you be healthy
May you be happy
May you live with ease

rooted

root - rooting - rooted

1. to grow roots or a root
2. to become firmly **established** or **settled**
3. to be the **source** or origin of
4. Root: give audible encouragement or applause to a contestant or team; cheer.

origin

"To take root" is from the 1530s as "**settle in the ground**," hence figurative use

Day 17: Rooted

The root chakra is located at the base of your spine. It is associated with red and helps ensure your
"basic human needs are met, creating a sense of emotional and physical stability."
Jilly Shipway, *Chakras for Creativity*

Today, I was fortunate to attend a learning opportunity focused on childhood attachment called Circle of Security (Powell, Cooper, Hoffman & Marvin, 2014). It's about creating a safe base so a child feels comfortable going out into the world to explore, knowing they'll have a supportive, welcoming person to return to. We continue this pattern throughout life. I held this in mind as I reflected on my week.

As a recovering people-pleaser, this week has been a bit challenging. Over the last nine months, I've spoken up about something important: focusing on seeing the humanity of all people and supporting inclusion. The roots go deeper, as many have called for this change for years. Although I feared risking relationships in this process, it actually helped me build community.

This week, a decision was made to support this change; some people are upset about it, and with me for speaking up about it. I'm grateful for the supportive base that holds me steady. This includes being rooted in my 'why' and being supported by many others in this work. I'm grateful for my mom, who has modeled how to stand up for something you believe in, for supportive family members, and for friends and community members who have gathered to continue the collective effort. Even though the winds may blow, I am confident in my roots of stable support.

Reflection Questions

What helps you feel grounded? Who helps you feel steady?

How can you invite stability into your day?

Did you have a secure base as a child? How are you supporting a secure base for young people in your life?

remember

remembered - remembering

1. to bring to mind or **think of again**
2. to **keep in mind** for attention or consideration
3. to retain in the **memory**

origin
mid-14c., *remembren*,
"**keep or bear** (something or someone) **in mind**, retain in the
memory, preserve **unforgotten**"

Day 18: Remember

Elephants are known for their superb memories. Their remarkable recall aids their survival as it helps them memorize migration routes, remember water sources, and support their social structure.

For elephants and humans alike, memories are stored not only in the mind but also in the body. Sights, smells, and sounds may elicit memories. We can feel them.

To re-member is to return to wholeness, embodiment, and presence. It also helps us hold each other in our minds and hearts.

Reflection Questions

What helps you remember your wholeness and worthiness?

Text or call a friend or family member you've been thinking about. How did that feel?

Is there a sound or a certain song that brings you immediately back to childhood?

Learn more about elephant memory: www.livescience.com/do-elephants-have-good-memories

wild

wildish - wildness

1. living in a **state of nature** and not ordinarily tame
2. not inhabited or cultivated
3. **not subject to restraint** or regulation

origin

Old English *wilde*
'in the **natural** state, uncultivated, **untamed**, undomesticated, **uncontrolled**"

Day 19: Wild

When I was a kid, my dad had horses on his farm. My horse was named April, and she had a diamond-shaped spitfire down her nose.

She was broken in, but her spirit wasn't broken. I didn't ride her much, but she wasn't wild either.

I used to love drawing her and any other horse, too. I imagined her free in a field of wildflowers and painted this picture.

Reflection Questions

How can you invite some freedom into your day?

Go barefoot outside. Feel the grass between your toes. What else do you notice?

What helps your inner wild child feel free?

ease

rMg

easeful - easy

1. to **free** from something that pains, disquiets, or burdens
2. to make less painful, **alleviate**
3. to maneuver **gently** or carefully
4. to make it **less difficult**

origin

c. 1200, "physical **comfort**, undisturbed state of the body;
tranquility, peace of mind,"

Day 20:  Ease

Today, I woke up at 3 am with my mind racing with all the day's to-dos. Luckily, I was able to fall back to sleep, but I still had an anxious feeling when it was time to get up.

I remembered a helpful meditation that asks you to consider "what if it were easy."

For me, it helps loosen the knots of expectation and trust the flow.

Meditation:https://insighttimer.com/dariusbashar/guided-meditations/what-if-it-were-easy-morning-meditation

Reflection Questions

What if it were easy?

How can you invite some ease into your day?

What helps you loosen the knots of expectation?

tranquil

rMq

tranquility

1. **free from agitation** of mind or spirit
2. **free from disturbance** or turmoil
3. **unvarying in aspect:** steady, stable

origin

from Latin **_tranquillus_**
"quiet, calm, still."

Day 21:  Tranquil

Lately, I've noticed that when I 'should' myself to do something, it ends up being a mess and more work in the long run.
When I couldn't think of a word to pair with this sweet barn I see occasionally, I decided not to force it. I'm trying not to 'should on myself.'
The word that finally came to mind for this painting was "tranquil."

Reflection Questions

How might you stop "shoulding" on yourself?

How can you invite tranquility into your day?

What helps your inner child feel calm?

sol

rMg

sun

1. the **luminous celestial body** around
   which the Earth and other planets revolve
2. the Roman god of the sun

origin

from Latin *sol* **"the sun"** + *sistere* **"stand still, take a stand;**
to set, place, cause to stand"

Reflection Questions

What invitations to shine bright are you leaning into?

Where do you find stillness?

How might you celebrate how far you've come?

Day 22:  Sol

*"May the long-time sun shine upon you,
all love surround you,
and the pure light within you,
guide your way on."*

- Kundalini Yoga song "Longtime Sun"

When there are no words.

This painting is dedicated to a sweet mama and precious babe who will have to say goodbye far too soon.
May love surround them and their family as their hearts break.
Sending love to all those who are grieving the loss of their wished-for babes. Your eternal connection is sacred.

Roses symbolize timeless love and beauty.

Day 23: no words

Reflection Questions

How do you sit with love so strong and grief so big?

How can you practice presence by showing up and "being with" someone who is grieving when there are no words that will take the pain away?

Can you feel the presence of those who are no longer earthside?

learn

learn - learning

1. to gain **knowledge** or understanding of or skill in by **study,** instruction, or **experience**
2. to come to **know**
3. to acquire knowledge or **skill** or a **behavioral tendency**

origin

Old English *leornian*
"to get **knowledge**, be cultivated;
study, read, think about"

Day 24: *Learn*

Reflection Questions

What do you love to learn about?

How can you invite curiosity into your day?

Practice having a beginner's mind to see something with a fresh perspective. What shifted?

This sweet red chair belonged to my husband's grandparents, who had it reupholstered with this amazing crushed red velvet material.
This is where I sit each morning to reflect, journal, and read.
One of my top strengths is the love of learning. Strengths Finder experts say, "Learners have the natural curiosity of learning experience that leads to ever-evolving paradigms and ever-expanding perspectives." (Liesveld, 2014)
This burning curiosity results in an energy rush and emotional boost, like a "learner high" with a strong urge to share information with others.
I also have "Input" as a top strength, which helps me sort through, organize, and distribute information.
I have to intentionally slow down to connect the dots between the knowledge gained to be accessible and useful.
This project has been a fun outlet for creativity and curiosity to bring them together, learn, and share.

Learn more about the CliftonStrengths Assessment at https://www.gallup.com/cliftonstrengths

grow

growth - growing

1. to increase in size by a natural process
2. to **expand**; gain
3. to develop and reach maturity
4. to be capable of growth; **thrive**
5. to come into **existence from a source**, spring up
6. to come to be by a gradual process or by degrees

origin

From Old English *growan* (of plants)
"to **flourish, increase, develop, get bigger**"

Day 25:  Grow

> **"Grounded and Growing"**
> by Rachel Gilbertson
>
> May you remain grounded in your worth,
> rooted to our interconnected nature,
> and nourished by unconditional love.
> May you stand tall in your wisdom and strength,
> cultivate courage and compassion,
> and radiate your essence to the world.
> May you be guided by intuition
> as you gracefully grow and
> beautifully bloom into your full potential.

Reflection Questions

What areas of life are you growing into?

How can you flourish today?

Think back to when you were a child. What/Who helped you become who you are today?

loved - loving

1. strong **affection** for another arising out of kinship or personal ties; **attraction** and **tenderness** felt by lovers.
2. warm **attachment, enthusiasm,** or **devotion**
3. a **beloved** person

origin

Old English *lufian*
"to feel **love** for, **cherish**, show love to;
delight in, approve,"

Day 26: Love

Today, my husband, Ben, and I celebrated our 18th wedding anniversary.
Reflecting back, I recall a conversation with a couple during our pre-marriage classes.
I can't remember their advice exactly, but it was something to the effect of marriage being about building a solid base while allowing each person to grow individually and together as a couple.
Like trees with strong roots of friendship, a solid trunk of love, and branches, each growing independently yet intertwined.
I'm grateful that our love has continued to grow over the years and also allowed for our family tree to expand with sweet sproutlings.
This is a painting to reflect our love, family tree, and this important lesson.

Reflection Questions

Who do you love?

Who nourishes your roots and supports your growth?

What does your family tree look like?

Day 27

playing - played

1. to occupy oneself in an activity for **amusement** or recreation;
2. to take part in a sport or **game**
3. to deal or **behave carelessly** or indifferently, especially for one's own amusement

origin

from Old English *plegan, plegian* "move lightly and quickly, occupy or busy oneself, **amuse oneself**; engage in active exercise; **frolic**; engage in **children's play**; make sport of, mock; perform music."

69

Day 27: Play

I'm grateful for my kiddos, who remind me to play.

"There is a strong connection between the practice of play and the emotional and cognitive development of the brain. So not only will engaging in play, which could include physical activity or sports, a creative practice such as painting, or simply giggling with your child, improve your physical and emotional well-being, but it can also reinforce patterns in your brain and optimize the learning process.

A life devoid of play faces significant health risks, such as depression, a decreased immune system, and stress-related diseases...Dr. Brown argues that incorporating more joyful, non-repetitive activities in our lives can replace these health and societal risks with a greater sense of well-being for ourselves and our communities" (Brown, 2011).

Reflection Questions

Did you play today?

How might you invite some amusement into your day?

What was your favorite thing to play as a child?

Learn more about the importance of play:
https://www.takingcharge.csh.umn.edu

70

persist eMg

persists - persisting - persisted

1. to be obstinately repetitious, **insistent**, or **tenacious**
2. to hold firmly and **steadfastly to a purpose**, state, or undertaking despite obstacles, warnings, or setbacks.
3. to continue in **existence**, last

origin

from Latin *persistere* "abide, **continue steadfastly**,"
from per "thoroughly" "forward," hence "through" + sistere
"**come to stand**, cause to stand still"

In Liz Gilberts' book, *Big Magic: Creative Living Beyond Fear*, she outlines the interconnections of courage, enchantment, permission, persistence, trust, and divinity within the creative process.

I'm continuing to notice how all of these show up for me. I'm also seeing how a daily commitment to my craft comes with challenges.

However, pursuing any endeavor or consistently showing up requires a degree of difficulty. Reflecting on how your tenacity and persistence have helped you in the past can be a powerful practice to help you overcome current obstacles.

Day 28:

Persist

"Nevertheless, She Persisted."

Reflection Questions

When have you not given up?

What have you achieved and overcome?
How did you care for yourself in the process?

What has your persistence done for you?

be

being - become - belong

1. **exist, live; take place; happen; to belong; attend**
   a. not be confused with <u>bee</u> - an insect, such as a
   bumblebee or honeybee; a community social
   gathering (spelling bee)

origin

Old English *beon, beom, bion*
"be, exist, come to be, become, happen"

Day 29: *Be*

How are you today?
Have you been a busy bee?
Have you buzzed around or bumbled about?
Did you take time to simply be?

Reflection Questions

What practices help support how you want to be?

When you were a kid, what did you want to be when you grew up?

What do you want to be now?

rain

1. **water falling in drops** condensed from vapor
   in the **atmosphere**
2. the **descent** of this water

origin

"Emotion:"
Latin roots (*e* -out and *movere* -motion)
Moving out or in motion, meaning that "emotions are moving".

Day 30: *Rain*

I recently told a friend I'm not very good at small talk because I can only talk about the weather for about half a second before I want to know the weather in your heart. Although trust is necessary to honestly answer that question, it sure beats the standard, "How are you?" followed by the socially acceptable responses of "good, fine, or busy."

Today, the weather in my heart is sad, rainy, scary, stormy. It's been a tough day on many levels.

Checking in with your feelings and being with difficult emotions is essential.

Below is a meditation practice developed by Tara Brach to help turn toward difficult feelings with R.A.I.N.

> **R: Recognize what is happening**
> **A: Allow the experience to be there**
> **I: Investigate with kindness**
> **N: Nurture with Self Compassion**

"You are the sky. Everything else is just the weather."

– Pema Chodron

Learn about radical compassion and try a RAIN meditation at www.tarabrach.com/rain

Reflection Questions

What is the weather in your heart today?

What emotions are coming up for you today?

What helps you acknowledge emotions, allow them to move through, and glean any gifts of wisdom they bring you?

"Be you, love you.
All ways, always."

— Alexandra Elle

prides - priding

1. the quality or state of being **proud,** such as reasonable **self-esteem**, **confidence,** satisfaction in oneself, **self-respect**
2. an event or series of events celebrating and affirming the **rights, equality, and culture of LGBTQ people**.

origin

The Old English form with -*te* probably is from or influenced by pride. Meaning "elated by some act, fact, or thing"
The sense of "**fearless or untamable spirit**"

Day 31: Pride

After another tough day, I'm holding onto hope. It seems natural that following a storm, there is the potential of a rainbow. A rainbow symbolizes hope and pride.

Many people are facing difficulties and are imagining a brighter future.

I want to live in a world where everyone is free to be their full self and is supported in designing the life of their dreams.

Reflection Questions

What are you proud of?

What supports you in being free to be your full self?

How do you recognize the full humanity in others?

boldly - boldness

1. **fearless** before danger; requiring or exhibiting **courage** or daring.
2. unduly forward and **brazen**; impudent
3. strikingly different, or **unconventional**
4. clear and distinct to the eye; strong or pronounced; prominent

origin

from Old English *beald, bald*,
"stout-hearted, brave, confident, strong,"

Day 32: *Bold*

The cherry red stood out boldly in comparison to the greens of the other trees.
As I started painting, the tree refused to be contained within the little black box.
It made me think of the phrase, "I can hardly contain myself!". And really, why should we 'contain ourselves' anyway?
It saddens me to think how often we contain ourselves and limit our potential. We have all learned to do this.
To stay small, blend in, and be the same.
However, what if we were all less contained and took big or baby steps into boldly being more of our whole selves? Can you imagine the bright, beautiful belonging that could be?

Reflection Questions

In what ways do you feel contained?

How might you invite some boldness into your day?

What bold moves might you take to step fuller into your being?

nostalgia

nostalgic

1. a **bittersweet longing** for things, persons, or situations of the past.
2. the condition of being **homesick**; homesickness.

origin

from Greek *algos*
"pain, grief, distress" *+ nostos* **"homecoming"**

Day 33: Nostalgia

I felt nostalgic seeing this photo of a barn that used to be on our family farm, so I decided to paint it.

Reflection Questions

What do you feel bittersweet longing for?

What do you experience now that you might feel nostalgic about in the future?

What smells bring you right back to childhood?

inspired - inspiring - inspires

1. to affect, guide, or arouse by **divine influence**.
2. to **fill with enlivening** or exalting emotion
3. to stimulate action; **motivate**
4. to draw in (air) by inhaling; to **breathe life into**

origin

Latin *inspirare* "blow into, breathe upon, breathe into"
from *in-* "in" + *spirare* "**to breathe**" (see **spirit**)

Day 34: Inspire

This 100-day project is teaching me so many lessons as I watch what unfolds by following curiosity, inspiration, and enchantment.

It's been fascinating to see what emerges each day as one spark of an idea ignites more insights over time. I'm noticing being tuned in more closely to what catches my eye, words that resonate, and themes that arise throughout the day.

Although I've been painting each day, I notice the words have been coming more slowly and sometimes not until the next day. Therefore, I'm a day behind. My inner critic and inner perfectionist like to remind me of this fact. However, grace continues to grant me permission to loosen up and not force it. Inspiration is ever-present, yet can be elusive.

This project has continued to teach me to trust inspiration and enchantment. They refuse to be rushed or forced. If they are, they lose their magic. This, too, is a lesson for me.

Reflection Questions

What and who inspires you?

How might you invite some inspiration into your day?

How does inspiration come to you? What does that feel like in your body?

A Mediation for Inspiration
by Rachel Gilbertson

*Take a posture that embodies dignity.
Growing tall in your strength and grounded in your presence.
Invite your belly to soften, allowing the breath to flow in and out freely.
Follow this gentle inhale....and this gentle exhale.
Remember that each time you take in air, you are inspired.
Inhale into any areas of discomfort
Exhale, creating space for the tension to loosen
Inhale fresh air and inspiration
Exhale creating a clearing for creativity
Inhale, fill yourself up
Exhale let go
Inhale smile
Exhale relax*

imagine

rMg

imagining

1. the act or power of forming a mental image of something not present to the senses or **never before wholly perceived in reality**
    a. **creative ability**, a creation of the mind
2. to have a notion of or about without adequate foundation; **fancy or believe**

origin

from Old French *imaginer*
"sculpt, carve, paint; decorate, embellish"

Day 35: Imagine

Just when I make peace with being a day behind on my 100-day project, inspiration shows up with an invitation to imagine. This is another lesson in trusting the process.

"Creativity is the act of turning new and imaginative ideas into reality. Creativity is characterized by the ability to perceive the world in new ways, to find hidden patterns, to make connections between seemingly unrelated phenomena, and to generate solutions."

Jilly Shipway, *Chakras for Creativity*

Reflection Questions

What do you imagine?

Could you take some time to daydream today? What comes up?

Where did your imagination take you as a child?

heart

heartfelt

1. the chambered organ that pumps blood
2. the **vital center** and source of one's being, emotions, and sensibilities.
3. capacity for **sympathy or generosity, compassion**
4. **courage; resolution; fortitude**

origin

Old English *hiertan* "**give heart to**,"
from late 14c. "seat of inmost **feelings**; will; especially **love and affection; courage.**"

Day 36: Heart

"Creativity, like a heartbeat, has a rhythm and a pulse. It alternates between periods of doing and times of simply being...
The heart chakra teaches you to show compassion and love yourself and others as you tread this creative path...
In order for your creativity to be heartfelt, it must come from a place of love. It is not a sentimental love; it is bold and courageous, a fighting force for justice, peace, equality, and a fairer world."

Jilly Shipway, *Chakras for Creativity*

Reflection Questions

What do you make from a place of love?

How might you share your gifts with the world?

The heart chakra is associated with unconditional love. How can you practice loving yourself and others unconditionally?

flow

flowed - flowing - flows

1. to move or run **smoothly** with unbroken
   continuity, as in the manner characteristic of a fluid.
2. to proceed **steadily** and **easily**
3. to exhibit a smooth or **graceful continuity**

origin

from Old Norse *floa* "to deluge,"
Old High German *flouwen* "**to rinse, wash**"

Day 37: Flow

This chakra is in your lower belly and pelvic area. It is associated with the color orange and helps you ride the ebb and flow of life and creativity. It helps us access a deep source of wisdom, our intuition. It supports us in enjoying life and following pleasure.

I often think about intuition and how it always comes before logic. Our Western culture has this so backward as we are trained to follow plans and justify things by how rational they are.
Instead, if we trust intuition and follow through, it all starts to make perfect sense. But only in retrospect. We must practice listening to that inner knowing and take baby steps toward trusting it will all work out okay.

I'm noticing my paintings are becoming more like this. It's a blank page and an inkling of an idea that only makes sense when finished.

Reflection Questions

What helps you find flow?

How might you invite some pleasure into your day?

Could you think back to a time you followed your intuition? What does that deep knowing feel like in your body?

confidence - confidently

1. full of conviction: **certain**
2. having or showing **assurance** and **self-reliance**

origin

from Latin *confidentem*
"firmly trusting, reliant, self-confident, bold, daring"

Day 38:

These lilies bloomed in our flower bed, and vibrant orange caught my eye.

"The meaning of the orange lily flower has been interpreted in different ways. It is generally thought of to represent emotions such as confidence and, at the extreme, pride."

In the Buddist tradition, tiger lillies symbolize compassion and mercy.

Within my work in wellbeing coaching and supporting behavior change, I've learned that confidence is strategically built over time with support.

Self-determination theory (Ryan & Deci, 2000) outlines the following as universal needs for psychological health and wellbeing:

- Autonomy - not feeling persuaded or controlled
- Competence - seeking confidence and mastery of a skill
- Relatedness - being connected to others and finding a sense of belonging.

As we create conditions for and seek out these elements of well-being, we also improve our self-efficacy.
Self-efficacy: The person's confidence in performing a particular behavior; Approach behavioral change in small steps to ensure success. As the person's confidence and expectations to succeed increase, the positive behavior will increase, and a behavior change will result (Marcus et al., 2006).

Reflection Questions

What helps you access a confident ease?

What area do you want to build confidence in? What small steps can you take to grow in this area?

Did you feel confident and carefree as a child? What can support you in feeling this way now?

unplugged - unplugging

1. to remove (a plug, such as an electric plug) from a socket
2. to **temporarily refrain from using electronic devices**
   (such as computers and smartphones)

origin

1775, from *un* "reverse, opposite of" + <u>plug</u>

Day 39: Unplug

My daughter, Sam, strongly recommended I paint an outlet today since I didn't include it in yesterday's lily painting. She said it probably felt left out. I thanked her for being inclusive to the needs of everything and agreed to paint an outlet.

It made me think about how I pretended inanimate objects were alive as a child. My daughter's request invited that sense of imagination and enchantment.

This came up: **Imagine shocked outlets at the audacity of the electric cord unplugging to take a break from all the energy.**

Reflection Questions

What helps you unplug?

What might help you overcome the cultural messages to resist rest?

Do you remember when we didn't have cell phones? What did you do to entertain yourself? Did you imagine inanimate objects were alive?

> **Mindfulness Tips with Technology:**
> - Notice how you feel before you engage with your smartphone, computer, social media
> - Notice how you feel as you are scrolling
> - Notice how you feel afterward

leap

leaped - leaping - leapt

1. to **spring free** from or to **jump** from the ground
2. to **pass abruptly** from one **state or topic** to another

origin

from Old English *hleapan*
"to jump, spring clear of the ground by force of an initial bound; run, go dance, leap upon"

Day 40: *Leap*

Forty days into this project, and I've been taking requests for inspiration

My oldest daughter, Taylor, suggested I paint the decorative frogs our neighbor puts out on a nearby rock. We live in the country, and this frog-clad rock is alongside a dead-end road. There is no purpose to displaying these frogs other than to delight the very few that pass by and notice, like us.

As I saw these frogs again, I imagined one contemplating leaping into unknown waters. What will it decide to do? What if there's no guarantee? Will it trust itself to take care of itself regardless of the outcome?

To leap or not to leap: that is the question.

Reflection Questions

What could you do for nothing more than sheer delight?

What area of your life are you contemplating leaping in?

When in your past have you made a leap into uncertainty? What happened?

enough

1. sufficient to meet a need or **satisfy a desire; adequate**

origin

Old English *genog*
"sufficient in quantity or number"

Day 41:  Enough

You know the story of "Goldilocks and the Three Bears," right?
This is a painting of the Inner Critic and the Three Bears.
It's a journey from "What if I'm too much?" or "What if I'm not enough?"
to "What if I'm just right?"

Reflection Questions

What does enough feel like?

How might you thank your inner critic for trying to protect you? Then, could you invite it to rest?

Repeat Stewart Smalley's affirmation: *"I'm good enough, I'm smart enough, and dog-gone-it, people like me!"* What came up as you said that?

Bear Drawing Inspiration and Tutorial: Christopher Hart on YouTube & Shutterstock, PaintingValley.com

plant

planted - planting

1. to put or set in the **ground for growth**
2. **establish**, institute
3. to place in or on the ground

origin

From the Latin *planta* "sprout, shoot, cutting"
from *planta* "**sole** of the foot"

Day 42: *Plant*

I made this first "Planting Seeds of
Loving Kindness Tree" in 2015.
This is even more special because I used
some of my Grandma Frances'
necklaces for the beads.
She was a gem of a lady, and she
modeled unconditional love. This tree is
a reminder to carry that love forward.

"Planting Seeds of Love & Kindness"
By Rachel Gilbertson

*When seeds of love and kindness are planted, strong roots begin to form
allowing us to be grounded in presence and connected to ourselves and each other.
By cultivating compassion and nurturing self-acceptance,
we grow into who we are and blossom into who we are becoming.
This creates space for others to do the same.
With tender care and some growing pains, our roots deepen, and a solid trunk is formed.
Both offer stability as winds of change blow through.
Our branches reach for each other, and our roots become intertwined
as we stand in our collective strength.
We transform with the seasons, show our true colors, and learn the art of letting go.
The cycle of grounding & growing and rooting & rising continues
as our seeds of love and kindness grow into connection and belonging.*

Reflection Questions

What are you planting?

How might you cultivate compassion and nurture self-acceptance?

What growing pains have you experienced that allowed your roots to deepen?

"We can imagine ourselves planting seeds
of kindness into the earth
with each step we take and
pausing long enough in presence
to add the warmth
those seeds need to sprout."

-Ruth King, *Mindful of Race*

open

rMg

openness

1. having **no enclosing or confining barrier**; accessible on all or nearly all sides
2. completely free from concealment; exposed to general view or **knowledge**

origin

From Old English *open*
"not closed down, **raised up**"

Day 43:  Open

When the crown chakra is open, you feel connected to something greater than yourself.
The crown chakra is located above the crown of your head. It is depicted as a thousand-petal lotus flower.

It represents consciousness, "*seeing the bigger picture, putting aside ego, connecting to the divine mystery and channeling its cosmic awareness into creativity...When the crown chakra is awakened, we feel a sense of being at one with the world.*"
Jilly Shipway, *Chakras for Creativity*

Reflection Questions

What helps you connect with something larger than yourself?

How might you invite wonder and awe into your day?

Go outside and look at the moon and stars. What do you notice? Do you "perceive yourself as a minuscule but precious part of an infinite universe?"

potential

1. the inherent ability or **capacity for growth**, development, or future success
2. **the possibility** that something might happen or result from given conditions

origin

The noun, meaning "that which is possible, **anything that may be**" from Middle English *potencies* "a caustic medicine"

Day 44: Potential

Reflection Questions

Imagine the potential of today by asking yourself: "I wonder what's going to happen today?"

What is your morning routine like? How might you incorporate things that make you feel awake and alive into your morning?

What has helped you grow into your potential throughout your life?

Is this a painting of rolling hills or rolling waves, or do you see something else? It's full of potential, and it's up to you. To me, it represents mornings. My favorite time of day. A fresh start full of possibilities and potential.

Sometimes, the possibilities fill up the day. That's what happened yesterday, so it got too late to share this. I am finding that I'm making my art in the evening because I haven't fit it into my morning.

I have a lovely morning routine that supports my self-care: meditating, journaling, working out, and then breakfast. It's space and time before the busyness and business of the day begins. I'm noticing that my daily painting emerges throughout the day as images catch my eye, words stand out, and themes bubble up. So, that's the process for now, even though part of me wants to find time to paint in the morning. We'll see how it continues to unfold...the possibilities are endless.

108

squirrelly

squirrel!

1. relating to, resembling, or characteristic of a squirrel
2. tending to be **unusually active, restless**

origin

from 1876, "**included to rush this way and that unpredictably**"

Day 45:

Squirrelly

I couldn't decide if today's word should be squirrel! or squirrelly, so I decided it could be both (as that seems fitting).

This idea popped into my head since there are days I feel downright silly and squirrelly.

There are also many times throughout the day when my attention needs to shift quickly from one thing to the next, and distractions can pop up.

Sometimes, these "squirrel!" moments are prompted by external events; sometimes, they're generated internally.

Reflection Questions

In what ways do you allow yourself to be silly and squirrelly?

What helps you limit distractions to keep your focus?

Do you think squirrels get distracted by dogs?

Day 46

Be > Do > Have

BE: Be present in the moment

DO: Practice mindful awareness and being present with others. Notice thoughts, feelings, and sensations in the moment.

HAVE: Improved connection with yourself and others

Day 46:

Do you think I'm going to tell you to behave?

Nope, definitely not.
But I am going to tell you about the
journey from be to have: BE → DO → HAVE.

> *"Often people attempt to live their lives backward: They try to have more things, or more money, in order to do more of what they want so that they'll be happier. The way it actually works is reverse. You must first be who you really are, then do what you really need to do, in order to have what you want." - Margaret Young*

Kate Northrup also outlines how this plays out in our culture of DO > HAVE > BE.
We are taught to achieve, earn gold stars, and strive to "do the right things" so we "get the right things" so we can "be happy/fulfilled/successful."

> EXAMPLE:
> **DO:** Go to school, get good grades
> **HAVE:** The job, buy the house, have the family
> **BE:** Think we'll be happy/fulfilled/successful

> EXAMPLE:
> **DO:** Go to the gym, go on the program/diet/ buy the gadget
> **HAVE:** The body you want/ lose X pounds
> **BE:** Think we'll be happy/fulfilled/successful/beautiful/worthy

This model always has us wanting more because once we achieve, we might feel momentary pride, success, or joy, but then we are always looking to the next thing to do or have so we can have that feeling again.

As Danielle LaPorte says, *"You're not chasing the goal itself- but the feeling that you hope attaining the goal will give you."*

BE > DO > HAVE

Therefore, if we gain clarity over how we want to be (how we want to feel, how we want to be), we can use that as our measuring guide to determine what we do, and finally have the feeling we've been longing for. This is where the process becomes the reward within itself, not the outcome of achieving the goal

Reflection Questions

BE: "How do I want to be at this moment?" How do I really feel? How do I want to be (in general or in a particular role/area in your life)?

DO: What action steps are required to cultivate qualities of how I want to be in my life? What am I already doing that supports how I want to be in my life (or this particular role/area)?

HAVE: What will I have if I cultivate this quality?

"You're not chasing the goal itself - but the feeling that you hope attaining the goal will give you."

- Danielle LaPorte

soothe

soothing

1. to please by or as if by **attention** or **concern**
2. **relieve, alleviate**
3. to bring **comfort**, **solace**, or **reassurance** to

origin

from Old English *sodian*
"show to be true, bear witness, offer confirmation"

Day 47: Soothe

Aloe vera is known for its soothing, moisturizing, and cooling properties. In some cultures, the aloe vera plant symbolizes beauty, good luck, and fortune. In other cultures, it is used for healing and protection. During the Victorian era, aloe vera plants were given to help heal grief.

Reflection Questions

What helps soothe you?

How do you offer comfort, solace, or reassurance?

How might you offer healing and protection for your inner child?

Learn more about Aloe Vera at https://naturalscents.net/

nurtured - nurturing

1. the action of **caring for offspring**
2. something that **nourishes, sustenance**

origin

from Old French *norture, nourreture*
"food, nourishment; education, training"

Day 48: Nurture

My hubby took this picture of a doe and her fawn in our woods a few weeks ago. The fawn was nursing when he saw them. He said they just looked up and continued what they were doing without getting scared.
When I saw the picture, the word nurture came to mind.

Reflection Questions

What or who nurtures you?

What do you do to nourish yourself?

How might you nurture your inner child?

voice

rMg

voiced - voicing

1. to **express in words; utter**
2. to **pronounce** with voice
3. a **wish, choice, or opinion** openly
   or formally expressed

origin

from Latin *vocem*
*"voice, sound, utterance, cry, call, speech,
sentence, language, word"*

Day 49:  Voice

The throat chakra "enables you to give voice to your creations and to communicate your vision." This chakra is located at your throat, is associated with the color blue, and supports communication and expressing emotion.

It helps you "know when to speak and when to remain silent, aids your capability of speaking truth to power, and directs anger creatively."

> *"When we are in the habit of perpetually biting our tongue and suppressing our feelings, the cost will be the sense of constriction in the throat and the communication chakra."*
> Jilly Shipway, *Chakras for Creativity*

I have had to do a lot of work to find my voice. Learning about the chakra energy system has helped immensely.

I am more aware that when that tension arises, I can more easily sit with difficult emotions to hear the messages they bring, and I can usually find the words to express what comes up.

Now, when I feel a constriction in my throat, I think,

"I must have something big to say."

Reflection Questions

Have you ever lost your voice? What helped you heal and find it again?

What matters to you? How might you use your voice?

In what ways did you express yourself as a child? Do you still express yourself in the same ways?

"Integrity is choosing courage over comfort;
Choosing what's right over what's easy;
And choosing to practice our values rather
than simply professing them."

- Brené Brown

settle

settled - settling

1. to come to **rest**
2. to **sink gradually**
3. to become **quiet**

origin

Middle English *setlen*,
**"Become set or fixed, stable or permanent;
seat, sink down, come down"**

Day 50: Settle

When this word kept popping up in conversation, I resisted it being a theme for a painting. I was thinking of it in terms of settling for something less than ideal. However, that is just one meaning of the word. 'Settling for' and 'settling in' are distinctly different.

Settling in can be about settling into your space and putting down roots. It can also be about settling a disagreement by finding common ground. Muddy water can also settle and become clear. In mindfulness, the practice of embodiment is settling into your body. As Sarah Blondin puts it, *"coming down from your head and into your heart."*

When I thought of that process, I imagined an hourglass filled with sand. If it's the sand of awareness, mine is often stuck in my head. I must let it slowly trickle down until it fills my body. The gravity of each grain of sand tethers me more to the earth. As I settle in, there is space for being, feeling, and breathing. The settling of the sand creates space for clarity.

Reflection Questions

What helps you drop down from your head and into your body?

What helps you feel settled in your space? Is there something you can do to your surroundings to invite settling in?

One practice that helps me get out of my head is checking the sensations in my feet. Try it. What do you notice?

rushed - rushing

1. to move **swiftly; hurry; haste**
2. to make a **sudden or swift** attack or charge
3. to flow or **surge rapidly**, often with noise

origin

the transitive sense of "**to hurry up** (someone or something), cause to go swiftly" is from 1850

Day 51: Rush

I always think of my dad whenever I hear the Alabama song: ♫♪♫

> *"I'm in a hurry to get things done /*
> *Oh, I rush and rush until life's no fun /*
> *All I really gotta do is live and die /*
> *But I'm in a hurry and don't know why..."*

When I was a kid, he always seemed in a hurry and had many things to do. Now, as an adult and parent, I get it. I have the urge to hurry most of the time, and my to-do list often seems endless.

I'm grateful to my dad, who taught me to have a good work ethic and to fill my days with things that I enjoy, even if they make me busy.

The past two weeks have been jammed-packed. With many good things, but just completely full. Even though I've been efficient with every moment of my day, I still have things that go undone on my to-do list.

We have a vacation, and some more time will be freed up on our calendars in August. In the meantime, I'm continuing to prioritize self-care and trying to practice presence by doing one thing at a time.

I am finding joy amidst the rushing flow of life.
It makes me think that even rivers have stretches of rushing waters, and others have a more calm flow. This, too, is life...

Reflection Questions

Are you in the rushing rapid waters or the calm flow of a river right now?

Does rushing give you an adrenaline rush?

Were you ever bored as a child? Do you ever get bored as an adult?

"I don't want to miss my life, and I don't want you to miss yours either."

- Rachel Gilbertson

befriended - befriending

1. to **behave as a friend to**
2. to **assist favor, help**

origin

"**act as a friend** to," 1550s, from be + friend (n.).

Day 52: Befriend

Asking, "Do you wanna be my friend?" is often how small children initiate a friendship with another child they just met, perhaps while running around at a playground.

Yet, in adulthood, it seems more complicated to form friendships. Busy schedules, many responsibilities, and other barriers get in the way. We know that positive relationships enhance our wellbeing, but finding the time to initiate, build, and maintain friendships takes effort. This weekend, we are camping with friends, and I'm reminded how important it is to be in good company with others.

Reflection Questions

How might you be a good friend to yourself today?

Reflect on your friendships. Who comes to mind? Could you reach out to them today?

How did you make friends as a child? How do you make friends as an adult?

bliss - blissfully

1. full of, marked by, or causing **complete happiness**

origin

late 12c., *blisfulle*, "**glad, happy, joyus**"

Day 53: Blissful

Reflection Questions

Who and what supports your evolution?

How might you invite some bliss into your day?

What transformations have you gone through since you were a child?

Monarch butterflies were often fluttering by while camping with friends this blissful weekend.

Monarch butterflies "represent strength, endurance, spirituality, trust, sustaining what they believe, transformation, and evolution."

Good friendships help support these, too.

Learn more about monarch symbolism:
www.wellandgood.com

compass r.Mg

compassed - compassing

1. to make a **circle of, surround, encircle**
2. a device used to determine geographic **direction**
3. to **understand, comprehend**
4. to **bring about**

origin

from Old French *compas*
"**circle, radius; size**, extent; pair of compasses"

Day 54: Compass

Have you ever noticed this combination of words?

Compass

Compassion

Passion

Reflection Questions

What helps give your life direction?

Who helps you have compassion?

What are you passionate about?

anchor

1. a device attached to a ship cast overboard to hold it in a **particular place**
2. a **reliable or principle support: mainstay**

origin

From Latin *ancora* "**an anchor**,"
The figurative sense of "**that which gives stability or security**" is from late 14c.

Day 55: Anchor

A myth of mindfulness is that the goal is to clear your mind. That just isn't possible, as it's the brain's job to think. Thoughts, emotions, and sensations will come and go. The practice of mindfulness is observing these. The breath can serve as an anchor to the present moment as we follow each gentle inhale and each gentle exhale.

Activity:
Take ten deep breaths. Notice what breath you're on when your mind starts to wander. Note that just becoming aware that your mind has wandered is a moment of mindfulness.

Reflection Questions

Without judgment, what do you notice about the activity above?

What helps anchor you to the present moment?

What is an intention that you stay tethered to?

load - unload

1. to perform the **act of unloading**
2. to **relieve of something burdensome, unwanted, or oppressive**
3. to give forth a **usually sudden angry outburst**

origin

from Latin *exoneratus*,
"remove a burden, discharge, unload"

Day 56: Unload

The washer was agitated on a mental spin cycle, trying to take a load off their mind.
The dryer tried to reduce the static by saying it deals with pressing concerns by waiting to see how things unfold.
Although it was a delicate subject, it seemed to iron things out without hampering the day.

Reflection Questions

What are you sorting through right now?

What is your process for unloading and unpacking things?

Can you think of any laundry puns?

regally

1. of or relating to a monarch; royal
2. belonging to or **befitting a monarch**
3. **magnificent; splendid**

origin

Old French *regal*, **"royal"**

Day 57: Regal

"Peacock symbolism communicates themes of beauty, self-expression, confidence, royalty, and spirituality... Peacocks have many meanings, including creativity, regrowth, and renewal."

Reflection Questions

What makes you feel regal?

How might you invite more self-expression into your day?

When have you experienced regrowth and/or renewal?

Peacock symbolism
www.mindbodygreen.com

optimism

1. of, relating to, or characterized by **optimism:**
feeling or showing hope for the future

origin

from Latin *optimum,*
"the greatest good"

Day 58: *Optimistic*

The meaning of sunflowers stems from their very nature - always facing the sun, they symbolize unwavering faith and constant orientation towards the light. This is why they are often associated with positivity, happiness, and optimism.

These sweet sunflowers came with our CSA pick-up this week. We serendipitously met Farmer John and Sunshine Kelly one day and have been grateful to know them ever since. They have an amazing farm and provide beautiful produce and flower bouquets.

Reflection Questions

What are you feeling optimistic about?

How might you invite more positivity into your day?

Have you ever met anyone that radiates warmth and light like sunshine? Consider reaching out to let them know.

For more information about Farm Sol and their CSA visit: www.farmsol.online
Sunflower symbolism from https://thursd.com/articles/meaning-symbolism-sunflower

serendipitous - serendipitously

1. the faculty of making **fortunate discoveries by accident**
2. the fact or **occurrence of such discoveries**

origin

"faculty of making **happy and unexpected** discoveries," a rare word before 20c

Day 59: Serendipity

This project has been a fascinating way to observe the creative process. Occasionally, I know exactly what I'm going to paint. It becomes crystal clear at some point in the day. Often, a theme bubbles up throughout the day, and all comes together as the day unfolds. Other times, I'm not exactly sure what to paint when I sit down at the end of the day. Just a tiny blank page staring back at me. Today, I had no clue. I just sat down and started doodling with watercolors, and this is what came up.

Serendipity is one of my favorite words. It is also one of my favorite things to notice. I often notice serendipity in an unexpected joy in the moment. Other times, I can see serendipity in the rearview. Had I not randomly done X, Y likely wouldn't have ever happened. Perhaps the latter is a combo of serendipity and synchronicity. It seemed like too important of a word for a random doodle. Yet, I couldn't think of a better way for it to show up.

Reflection Questions

What is the last serendipitous event you recall?

How might you invite more serendipity into your day?

How do you notice serendipity showing up for you? Do you sense when it's happening in the moment or only through reflection?

glorious

glorious

1. having or **deserving glory**
2. conferring or **advancing glory**
3. **great beauty and splendor**
4. **delightful; wonderful**

origin
Old French *glorieus*
"glorius, blessed"

Day 60: Glorious

Sixty days into this 100-day creative endeavor. One of the most important gifts it has given me is to be on the lookout for ordinary moments that feel extraordinary. This was one such glorious moment.

Reflection Questions

How do you see the extraordinary in the ordinary?

Did you notice anything glorious today? What was it? What made it so?

What is one important lesson you have been gifted in your life?

luck

lucky - luckily

1. the **chance happening of fortunate fortune**
2. **good fortune** or **prosperity; success**
3. one's personal **fate or lot**

origin

probably from early Middle Dutch *luc*,
"happiness or good fortune"
a word of unknown origin.

Day 61: Luck

"Rabbits almost always symbolize prosperity, abundance, good luck, and fertility. Rabbit symbolism is consistent, unlike many other animals, which have different meanings in different cultures."

Reflection Questions

When have you felt lucky lately?

How might you practice gratitude in a way that feels meaningful to you?

What good fortune have you experienced in your life?

secure

secured - securely

1. **free from danger; affording safety**
2. easy in mind: **confident, assured sense**
3. able to **reliably afford or access** what is needed to **meet one's basic needs**

origin

Latin securus, of persons,
"free from care, quiet, easy,"

Guest Artist

Leo Gilbertson

Today, I have quite a treat for you...

I'm sharing this bonus painting featuring a very special guest artist, Leo, my 9-year-old son. Creating alongside my kids and sharing this process has been delightful.

I'm grateful for my family's support, interest, and involvement in this little artistic endeavor. I love it when they ask me what I'm going to paint, give suggestions for what I could create, ask if it's time for me to make my 'tiny little paintings,' and sometimes join in the fun.

Reflection Questions

What gives you roots and wings?

"A bird sitting on a tree is never afraid of the branch breaking, because her trust is not on the branch but on its own wings. Always believe in yourself."

-Charlie Wardle

What helps bolster your confidence?

Did you have access to things to meet your basic needs as a child? Did you have positive people to form secure attachments with? Do you now?

150

dabble

dabbled - dabbling

1. **to undertake an activity casually**
2. **spatter or splash**

No to be confused with:

1. **dapple** - mottled or spotted marking

origin

from 1550s, **"to dip a little and often,"**
hence, "to wet by splashing,"

Day 63: Dabble

The dappled ladybug delightfully dabbled daily.

Say that five times fast...

Reflection Questions

What do you like to dabble in? What are your hobbies?

Sit under a tree and notice the sunlight dappling through. What else do you notice?

As a child, did you enjoy patterns like polka dots? Do they still bring you joy?

Day 64

bubbly

bubblier - bubbliest

1. full of **bubbles: effervescent**
2. full of or showing **good spirits: lively, effusive**

origin

a bubble is a **"small vesicle of water or some other fluid inflated with air or gas,"** early 14c.,
perhaps from Middle Dutch *bobbel* (n.) and/or German *bubbeln*.

Day 64: Bubbly

I thought it would be fun to paint some bubbles today. Inspiration for each daily painting just sort of bubbles up throughout the day.

Sometimes, it's a crystal clear idea all at once; other times, it's extremely subtle and feels like a stretch to pull it all together.

Reflection Questions

When do you feel most bubbly?

How are you today? What is bubbling up for you?

Play in bubbles. What do you notice?

154

held

rMg

hold - holding

1. **to bear, sustain, or support** with or as if with the hands or arms.
2. to **keep in the mind; believe**
3. to **regard; consider**

origin

From Old English *healding* meant **"keeping, observance."**

Day 65: *Held*

I noticed this sweet farm is beautifully held into focus by branches from afar. It made me wonder what kind of memories that farm holds and how, even from a distance, trees are holding it, too.

Not the holding of a forced restraint but a gentle holding of space for rest and renewal.

In my work supporting the wellbeing of children and families, home visitors partner with families as the caregiver(s) and child(ren) form secure attachments through positive interactions.

We use the parallel process of reflective practice—a form of holding space to support collective wellbeing.

A child must be held physically, emotionally, and in many other ways.
 For the caregiver to do this important holding, they, too, must be held and supported.

Having a support system to hold them, and all holding each other, is what collective care is all about.

As they say, it takes a village to raise a child. I'd add that we all need each other across our lifetimes, too.

> "A broken family is a family in which any member must break herself into pieces to fit in. A whole family is one in which each member can bring her full self to the table knowing that she will always be both held and free."
>
> - Glennon Doyle

Reflection Questions

Where do you feel both held and free? By whom?

Who do you hold in your mind and support?

Who were your collective caregivers as a child?

"Everyone deserves the experience
of existing in someone else's mind.
It seems to me that this is
one of life's greatest privileges.
Possibly, though, there is one exception,
and that is the privilege of
holding another in one's own."

-Jeree Pawl

flash

flashed - flashing - flashes

1. to **burst forth** into or as if into flame
2. to **give off light** in sudden or intermittent bursts
3. to **appear or occur suddenly**
4. to move or **proceed rapidly**

origin

From Middle English *flashen*, *flasken*
"sprinkle or splash (water, powder, etc.)

Day 66:

The kids requested that I paint "Flash," their new cricket friend they met, tubing down a river.

Reflection Questions

What inspires and energizes you to jump into working on a new idea or project?

How do you integrate both times that require speediness and times of intentional slowing?

Did you make friends with critters when you were a child? Do you still?

serene

rMg

serenity

1. **content or composed; untroubled**
2. unaffected by disturbance; **calm or peaceful**
3. **unclouded; fair**

origin

From Latin *serenus*
"peaceful, calm, clear, unclouded"

Day 67: Serene

We recently returned from a weeklong trip to Wisconsin Dells. We had a lot of fun.

I was grateful to stay in this VRBO called "A Barn Good Time."

This quiet and serene space was just what we needed before and after a day of activities and adventures.

Serendipitous Update: this image is now hanging in "A Barn Good Time!"

Reflection Questions

Where do you feel most serene?

How might you invite some serenity into your day?

Has your need for quiet or serene spaces changed over your lifetime or remained consistent?

glide

rMg

glided - gliding - glides

1. to move in a **smooth, effortless manner**
2. to move silently and furtively
3. to occur or **pass imperceptibly**
4. to fly without propulsion from wings or an engine

origin

From Old English *glidan*

"move along smoothly and easily; glide away, vanish; slip, slide"

163

Day 68: Glide

This is "Fred the Goldfish," as requested and named by Leo.
Painting this made me think about how it feels to be gliding underwater.

Submerged and supported by the water surrounding you.

We recently went swimming when it was raining (without lightning). Being underwater and hearing the raindrops hitting the surface sounded magical. Have you ever tried it?

Reflection Questions

What might you do today to set you up to glide through tomorrow?

What things seem to come easily to you but are more difficult for others? How might you harness those natural gifts and talents?

Did you have a goldfish (or several) growing up? Do you have a goldfish now?

drift

drifted - drifting - drifts

1. to be **carried along** by currents of air or water
2. to proceed or move **unhurriedly or aimlessly**
3. to live or behave **without a clear purpose or goal**

origin

From late 16c.
"to float or be driven along by a current"

Day 69: Drift

As a child, when I tried to fall asleep, I imagined my bed floating in space while I drifted off. It was never scary, only peaceful gliding among the stars with moonlight as my nightlight. I still think of this from time to time at bedtime.

Lately, I've been thinking about how sleep is critical to our wellbeing. When I don't sleep well or enough, it impacts everything. A lack of sleep alters my energy level; my access to presence and patience with other people; choices for my own wellbeing (i.e. food, movement, etc); and my capacity for everything.

Reflection Questions

What rituals and routines do you have to let your body and mind know it's time for sleep?

How might you promote and protect your sleep?

As a child, what helped you drift off to sleep? How do you fall asleep now?

good

good

1. **being positive or desirable in nature;** not bad or poor
2. having the desirable qualities: of high-quality
3. **not spoiled or ruined**
4. superior to the average; satisfactory
5. of moral excellence, kind, loyal, well-behaved, proper
6. **worthy of respect, competent, reliable**

origin

From Old English *god* (with a long "o")
"excellent, fine; valuable; desirable, favorable, beneficial; full, entire, complete,"

Day 70: Good

In my work in Family Home Visiting, we have a reflective practice, which helps home visitors process the important work being done in partnership with families and how the home visitor experiences it. This process helps to support our individual and collective wellbeing.

Yesterday, during our check-in, we discussed how we were labeled as babies. Words like "good, fussy, spoiled, perfect, difficult, etc." came up. We also discussed how some of those labels stuck over time.

I thought about being a 'good' baby and how it has been important to me to be a' good' grown-up, too.

However, our standards seem to change over time. I thought about how babies are considered "good" when they sleep and/or eat well. Yet, as adults, we don't get praised for those very things.

Quite the opposite, actually.

Many in Western culture consider a lack of sleep a badge of honor. Slowing down, resting, and sleeping are not praised.

When we are offered food or desserts, we might even consider them "bad" foods and politely decline them with the refrain: "No, thank you, I'm good."

You ARE GOOD regardless of accepting or declining the goodies (which are also just food and not good or bad).

Day 70

As I was sharing this in conversation with others, additional examples of "Nope, I'm good, thanks!" came up:

"Would you like some goodies?"
"Nope, I'm good, thanks."

"Can I give you a hand with that?"
"Nope, I'm good, thanks."

"Are you hurt?"
"Nope, I'm good, thanks."

I'm working on shifting my responses to:

"That looks delicious, but I'll pass (or yes, please!).'"

"Yes, thank you for your help."

"Ouch, that did hurt. Thanks for asking."

The truth is, we ARE ALREADY GOOD, regardless of these choices. Perhaps saying "I'm good" is a subliminal way we constantly remind ourselves that we are good and worthy just as we are.

"I'm good enough, I'm smart enough,
and dog-gone-it, people like me!"

-Stewart Smalley

Reflection Questions

What labels were you given as a baby?

How have these labels continued, or not, as you grew?

How might you remind yourself and others of our inherent goodness?

Consider writing your inner child a letter reminding them they are "perfectly imperfect."

transitions

rMg

transitioning - transitioned

1. a change or **shift from one state, subject, or place, to another**; a period, phase, or process in which such a **change or shift is happening**

origin

From Latin *transitionem*
"a going across or over"

Day 71: Transitions

Fall is coming.
Leaves are starting to fall.
The morning air is more crisp.

I found this leaf the other day, and it is making me think of transitions.
Transitions are important. Some are big and noticeable, while others are small and subtle.
Lately, I've been paying more attention to transitions and trying to leave lots of space for
adjusting. I always tend to rush from thing to thing, place to place.

I'm working on slowing down.

My mantra this week has been, "I refuse to rush." I'm noticing how that helps relieve the
pressure and protect more time for transitioning from all things (tasks, topics,
transportation, etc).

Reflection Questions

How are you feeling about the upcoming seasonal transition?

Could you leave space for transitions, big and small? What do you notice?

How did you handle transitions and change as a child? How do you handle them now? What
helps you adjust?

simplify

rMg

simplifyed - simplifying

1. to **reduce in complexity** or extent
2. to **reduce to fundamental parts**
3. to make **easier to understand**

origin

from French simplifier "**to make simpler**"

Day 72: Simplify

This 100-day project has been teaching me so much.

It is an opportunity to observe the thoughts, feelings, beliefs, and behaviors related to creating something every day. These thoughts, feelings, beliefs, and behaviors are also reflected in life.

One of these lessons I'm reminded of is to simplify and leave space. It's so easy to add a little more to paintings each day. I notice that my paintings rarely have much blank space, and neither does my calendar or to-do list.

The phrase "don't overdo it" came to mind as I was painting recently. This is my attempt to do less because more isn't always better.

Reflection Questions

Do you tend to overdo it?

How might you simplify something in your life?

As a child, when you colored, did you like to color inside or outside the lines? Did you shade in each inch or leave some blank space?

seasons

1. a time characterized by a **particular circumstance or feature**
2. **period of the year** characterized by or associated with a particular activity or phenomenon
3. **one of the four quarters** into which the year is commonly divided

origin

from Old French *seison, seson, saison*
"season, date; right moment, appropriate time"

Day 73: Seasons

🎶 To everything turn, turn, turn
There is a season turn, turn, turn
And a time to every purpose under Heaven 🎶

Turn! Turn! Turn!
-The Byrds

Reflection Questions

What season of life are you in right now?

How might you invite ease into transitions?

What was your favorite season as a child? What is it now?

insight

insight

1. the power or act of **seeing into a situation**
2. the act or result of **apprehending the inner nature of things or of seeing intuitively**

origin

c. 1200, *innsihht,*
"sight with the 'eyes' of the mind, mental vision, understanding from within"

Day 74:  Insight

This chakra is located above and between your eyebrows. It is associated with indigo and helps you access insight, inspiration, and imagination.

> *"Working with the third eye chakra develops your intuition, clairvoyance, and imagination. You learn to see with your inner eye, visualize what it is you wish to create...*
>
> *Artists often express something that is just out of sight for the rest of us, and their work is a revelation helping others see more clearly...*
>
> *Regardless of whether you are involved in the arts or the sciences, working with this chakra opens you to the possibility of making creative leaps of intuition, resulting in innovation."*
>
> Jilly Shipway, *Chakras for Creativity*

Reflection Questions

Think back to when you had an insight or thought up something innovative. What happened?

How does your intuition get your attention?

What did you imagine as a child? What do you daydream about now?

kismet

kismet

1. a hypothetical force or personified power that **determines the course of future events**
2. **an inevitable and often bad outcome, condition, or end** that a particular person or thing will experience.

origin

from Turkish *qismet*
"portion, lot, fate" from root of quasama

Day 75:  Kismet

As I looked for synonyms for 'good fortune,' the word 'kismet' popped up as an option. It caught my attention and became the word of the day.

Reflection Questions

Do you believe in fate/destiny?

When did you last notice synchronicity in your life or a meaningful coincidence in your day? What happened?

As a child, did you have superstitious practices or rituals for good luck? Do you now?

notion

1. a belief or opinion
2. a mental image; an **idea or a conception**
3. an **impulse or whim**
4. small lightweight items for household use, such as needles, buttons, and thread.

origin

from Latin *notionem*
"concept, conception, idea, notice"

Day 76:  Notion

When I was little, I used to watch "Sewing with Nancy" on PBS. Nancy made beautiful quilts, and there was a segment called "Nancy's Notions" in which she talked about little sewing gizmos.

Notions also mean a belief, idea, or concept. It can also mean doing something on a whim.

As I was thinking of what to paint, a lightbulb appeared to signify an idea. Then, when I was sketching it, I started to see a hot air balloon. After I finished painting and writing this, I noticed it looked like the fabric was quilted. I imagined it was made by Nancy using her notions. It's so fun to watch a notion unfold and develop through art.

Reflection Questions

What mental images or ideas have you created into a concept?

Do you ever do anything on an impulse or whim?

Did you collect any notions or other small items as a child? Do you now?

182

envelop

enveloped - enveloping

1. **to wrap around; enfold; hide; enclose**

Not to be confused with:
<u>Envelope</u> - a flat paper cover or wrapper

origin

from Old French *envoleper, envoluper*
"envelop, cover; fold up, wrap up"

Day 77:  Envelop

I remember watching my grandma cook and bake in her kitchen when I was young. She never followed a recipe, just a pinch of this and a sprinkle of that. One day, I remember sitting at her counter, taking notes as I tried to capture her special recipes.

I also remember asking her about life, hoping to gain a few generations of wisdom in one afternoon. I don't recall what she said, even though I'm sure it was important. Looking back, I think I wanted to skip the lessons I had to learn on my own. Although we might want to know 'the answers' from others, we need to find them ourselves.

Regarding the image, this made me think of how we fold in ingredients and letters and can be 'in the fold' with others. We put letters in an envelope, push the envelope, and can also envelop someone in a hug and with support.

Reflection Questions

What are the ingredients that support your wellbeing?
What amounts of these do you need to feel your best? (i.e., sleep, movement, connection, etc.)

If you were to write a letter to your younger self, what wisdom would you share?
What advice would you give the 5, 15, or 20-year-old you?

How might you envelop your inner child with love?

intrigue

intrigued - intriguing

1. to **arouse the interest, desire, or curiosity** of
2. to get, make, or accomplish by **secret scheming: trick**

origin

from Italian *intrigare*
"to plot, meddle; perplex, puzzle"

Day 78: Intrigue

Today, I noticed that mountains kept appearing in images throughout the day. Curiosity asked me to look a little closer; intrigue inspired me, and creativity called me to create.

> *"Mountains symbolize constancy, eternity, firmness, and stillness. They have been used to represent the state of full consciousness...*
>
> *It often serves as a cosmic axis linking heaven and earth and providing "order" to the universe. Mountains evoke a special sense of awe and power, and no single image or meaning can capture or express every facet of its symbolic significance."*
> *- W.Y Evans-Wentz*

Mountains are also metaphors used in mindfulness practice. Jon Kabat-Zinn writes, *"Through it all, the mountain just sits, experiencing change in each moment, constantly changing, yet always just being itself. It remains still as the seasons flow into one another and as the weather changes moment by moment and day by day, calmness abiding all change..."*

Check out this 20-min Guided Mountain Meditation:

https://palousemindfulness.com/meditations/mountain.html

186

Reflection Questions

What intrigues you?

What helps you stay still and grounded?

Remind yourself that you are fully capable, creative, and complete, just as you are. What do you notice as you remind yourself of your wholeness?

"Curiosity is the compass that leads us to our passions. The future belongs to the curious."

-Anonymous

decide

decided - deciding

1. **to conclude or form a judgment or opinion** about (something) by reasoning or consideration
2. to reach a decision, **make up one's mind**

origin

from Latin *decidere*
"to decide, determine," literally "**to cut off**"

Day 79: Decide

Along with this 100-day creative challenge, I'm also doing a 100-day workout challenge called "Morning Meltdown." This morning, the instructor, Jericho McMatthews, said, *"If you want to create change on the outside, you gotta make it happen on the inside first. That means you have to make up your mind. Make it up!...and don't ever let yourself quit."*

As soon as I heard 'Make up your mind,' I imagined this image of a **made-up mind making up its mind.**

Reflecting on how to make up minds, I notice how much indecision frustrates me. I've been working on both patience and trust when it comes to this. Patience to allow space for others to decide for themselves and trust that we can adjust as needed, regardless of what is decided.

We want to make the "right" decision, but all the options usually have pros and cons. Making the best decision with the information we have at the time and trusting ourselves to navigate as needed has been a theme personally and professionally.

Reflection Questions

What do you need to make up your mind about?

What is your decision-making process?

How might you invite trust as you decide and navigate afterward?

patience

patient

1. **capacity of calm endurance;** forbearance

origin

from Old French *pacience*
"patience; sufferance, permission"

Day 80:  Patience

Do you ever wish you had a deep well of patience?
I am trying to cultivate this well, but sometimes it's deep, and other times it runs dry.

Patience is said to be a virtue and a form of wisdom. It's also one of the 9 Attitudes of Mindfulness. (Kabat-Zinn, 1990)

Reflection Questions

What helps you have a deep well of patience?

What sensations or signals show up to let you know your patience is running low?

How might you offer yourself compassion when you lose your patience? How can you practice repairing ruptures within relationships when this happens?

Patience:
✦ Letting things unfold in their own time
A child may try to help a butterfly emerge by breaking open a chrysalis, but the butterfly probably won't benefit from this help.

✦ Being completely open to each moment, accepting its fullness, knowing that, like the butterfly, things will emerge in their own time.
We should practice patience with ourselves. "Why rush through some moments to get to other 'better' ones? Each one is your life in that moment."

✦ Remind ourselves that there is no need to be impatient with ourselves. Much of the time, our thoughts overwhelm our perception of the present moment, causing us to lose our connection to it.

local

1. characterized by or relating to **position in space**
2. primarily serving the needs of a **particular limited district**
3. involving or affecting only a **restricted part of the organism**

origin

from Late Latin *localis*
"pertaining to a place"

Day 81: Local

We spent the weekend in one of my hometowns.

There were moments of nostalgia and reflection mixed in while making new memories.

This sweet building, which used to be a local bakery, caught my eye. I thought about how much history it held and the stories it stored, as we all do.

Reflection Questions

Where is your hometown? What do you miss about it? What don't you?

What are some of your favorite local stores? How do you support them?

What is one of your favorite childhood memories in the town(s) you grew up in?

nestle

nestled - nestling - nestles

1. to settle **snugly and comfortably**
2. to lie in a **sheltered position**
3. **to draw or press close,** as in affection; snuggle

origin

from Old English *nestlian*
"build a nest, make or live in a (bird's) nest"

Day 82: Nestle

As I've shared before, I rarely know what will come up when I sit down to paint or write.

As this cute bird emerged, it seemed fitting to give it a comfy nest to settle into.

As I thought about the word 'nestle,' this memory popped up: When I was little and stayed with my grandma, she'd tuck me into bed saying, "snug as a bug in a rug." That sweet ritual made me feel safe, settled, and loved.

The image of a bug snug in a rug might be a fun painting for another day.

Reflection Questions

Who and what makes you feel nestled in and cozy?

What was your bedtime routine as a child? What is it now?

Did you have a special item that made you feel safe and snuggly as a kiddo (blanket, stuffed animal, etc.)?

wise

1. **ability to discern** inner qualities and relationships: insight
2. accumulated philosophical or scientific learning: **knowledge**
3. **a wise attitude, belief, or course of action**

origin

from Old English *wisdom*
"knowledge, learning, experience"

Day 83: Wisdom

> *"We are learning to listen to the intelligence of our hearts and act on that wisdom."* -Danielle Laporte

Reflection Questions

What helps you access your inner wisdom? What are some signals of your body's wisdom?

How do you practice discernment?

Do you remember Owl from Winnie the Pooh or Mr. Owl from the Tootsie Roll commercial? What memories do they bring up for you?

snug

snuggle

1. **fitting closely and comfortably**
2. **enjoying or affording warm secure shelter or cover** and opportunity for ease and contentment
3. **offering safe concealment,** secure privacy

origin

from Old Danish *snog*
"neat, tidy"

Day 84:  Snug

*To follow the flow of inspiration, see Day 82

When I was little and stayed over with my grandma, she'd tuck me into bed, saying, "Snug as a bug in a rug." That sweet ritual made me feel safe, settled, and loved.

Today, my kids saw this painting, and I shared this story. They reminded me that I often used to say this phrase when I tucked them in as toddlers, too.

Reflection Questions

What makes you feel like a bug snug in a rug?

Do you have access to a warm and secure shelter? If so, what specifically about it provides you opportunities for ease and contentment?

Do you remember Glo Worms, the light-up stuffed animal? Did you have one as a kid?

morph

morphed - morphing - morphs

1. **to undergo transformation**
2. **enjoying or affording warm, secure shelter or cover**
   and opportunity for ease and contentment
3. **offering safe concealment**, secure privacy

origin
from Greek *metamorphosis*
"a transforming, a transformation"

Day 85:

On Day 5 of this project, I painted "Emerge," and on Day 85, it morphed and emerged again.

Did you know:
"Matrescence is the process of becoming a mother. It describes the all-encompassing physical, psychological, and emotional changes people go through on their journey to motherhood. Medical anthropologist Dana Raphael first coined the term 'Matrescence' in 1973 to describe the process of becoming a mother."

Similarly, 'patrescence' is the birth of a parent and signifies transforming into this new way of being.

Reflection Questions

How have you morphed over the course of your life? What changes have you undergone?

How might you invite compassion for all the versions of yourself?

Who are you becoming?

Learn more about Matrescence: https://cradlewise.com/blog/matrescence-your-birth-as-a-mother

empower

rMg

empowered - empowering

1. to give **official authority** or legal power to
2. **enable**
3. **to promote the self-actualization or influence of**

origin

from 1650s "impower" assimilated form of <u>en-</u> (in) + <u>power</u>
(pouer) **"ability; ability to act or do; strength, vigor, might,"**

Day 86: Empower

Butterflies continue to emerge as a theme throughout this project. They are a symbol of transformation, hope, and empowerment.

Speaking of empowerment, check out Empower Possible, LLC, to learn more about my pal Julie's work of helping others feel empowered as they made positive changes.

Julie Zaruba Fountaine is a certified change management specialist who uses a holistic approach encompassing wellbeing, self-development, social networking, and systems transformation.

I leave every conversation with Julie feeling more inspired and empowered. Learn more at: www.empowerpossible.com.

Reflection Questions

What helps you feel empowered?

What enables your sense of internal strength, vigor, and might?

Remind yourself that you are magic just as you are, capable of more than you can imagine. What do you notice?

create

rMg

creates - creating - created

1. to cause to exist; **bring into being**
2. to **give rise to**; produce
3. to produce through **artistic or imaginative effort**

origin

from Latin *creatus*
"to make, bring forth, produce, procreate, beget, cause"

Day 87: Create

Dear Creativity,
Is there anything you want to share with me?

Creativity:
Keep doing what you are doing
Show up and share
Watch the unfolding - it matters.
Trim down the critic's voice and focus on who it resonates for.
Do it for you.
Be in the messy middle.
Remember that how you do anything is how you do everything.
Align your ideas and find clarity.
They will work in concert.
Trust the emerging and unfolding glimpses of inspiration.

Back in January, I wrote this reflection after listening to this mediation:

"Creativity is a Relationship" by Darius Bashar on the Insight Timer app.
https://insighttimer.com/dariusbashar/guided-meditations/creativity-is-a-relationship

Reflection Questions

What does creativity want to share with you?

What do you want to create?
...or what are you currently creating?

How can you create a space that welcomes creativity?

gentle

gentler - gentlest

1. **considerate or kindly in disposition;** amiable and tender
2. not harsh or severe; **mild and soft**
3. **easily managed** or handled; docile
4. not steep or sudden; **gradual**

origin

from Old French *gentil/jentil*
"high-born, worthy, noble, of good family; courageous, valiant; fine, good, fair"

Day 88:  Gentle

After a busy few weeks (and months)... we
recently had some downtime.
It was a lovely reset for rest and rejuvenation.
A gentle reminder to slow down.
A reminder to be gentle.

Reflection Questions

How might you invite some gentleness into today?

What can you take off your to-do list today? Consider creating a to-don't list.

What reminders help you to be gentle with yourself and others?

intent - intend

1. what one intends **to do or bring about**
2. a **determination to act in a certain way**, resolve
3. **import; significance**
4. a process or manner of **healing of incised wounds**

origin

from Old French *entencion*
"intent, purpose, aspiration; will; thought"

Day 89: Intention

> *"Just as an acorn holds the potential to become an oak tree, we already possess the capacity to awaken."*
> -The Yoga-Sutra of Patanjali

Research has shown that mindful awareness combines Intention, Attention, and Attitude (Shapiro et al., 2006).

Through my work with *Art of Presence*, I've built upon this model also to include Action and Impact because when you focus on how you want to be, it changes what you do and how you do it.

The *Art of Presence* is discovering how these components interact and support one another. I'll feature one of these elements with a painting each day as I near the end of this 100-day project:

Intention: Cultivating awareness on purpose (and returning to it again and again...)

Setting an intention for how we want to feel, how we want to be, and how we want to show up in the world purposefully focuses our attention, aligns our attitude, and moves us toward inspired action.

It also helps us build our reflective capacity. In times when our impact doesn't match our intent, we have an opportunity to make amends and work to heal wounds and old patterns.

Reflection Questions

What seeds of intention are you planting?

What supports you in feeling/being this way?

How will you know if your intent matches your impact?

"Mindfulness means paying attention in a particular way: on purpose, in the present moment, and non-judgmentally."

-Jon Kabat-Zinn

attend to

1. the act or state of **applying the mind to something**
2. **observation; notice**
3. an act of **civility or courtesy,** especially in courtship

origin

from Latin *attentionem*
"attention, attentiveness,"
stem of *attendere*
"give heed to," literally **"to stretch toward"**

Day 90: Attention

As I've been doing this 100-day project, I noticed that I'm more likely to spot delightful things in my day-to-day life. The intention to paint daily subtly shifts my attention.

The other day, this sweet window and flower box caught my attention for a split second. I only caught a glimpse but knew I wanted to paint it. As I did, it came back in full focus.

Similarly, we can focus on what is important throughout our day by aligning our intentions with our attention. We might get distracted, but it's all about bringing our focus back again and again.

Attention: Pay attention to what is occurring in the present moment.

Bring close, compassionate attention to thoughts, feelings, and bodily sensations to learn from them and your inner wisdom.

You can slow down to more fully engage in the present moment.

Reflection Questions

What captivates your attention?

How might you align your intention with your attention today?

What distracts your attention from what you want to focus on? How might you minimize distractions?

"Your presence is your power.
Your presence is your freedom.
Your presence is your happiness."

- Sarah Blondin

attitude

1. a **position assumed** for a specific purpose
2. a **ballet position** similar to the arabesque in which the leg is bent at the knee
3. a **mental position, feeling, or emotion about** a fact or state

origin
from Italian *attitudine*
"disposition, posture"

Day 91: *Attitude*

Attitude:

✴ You are allowed to feel all of your feelings.
Being present with emotions actually helps them move through.

✴ Did you know that the Latin roots of emotion (e-out and motion-movere) Move out or In motion, which means that emotions are moving?

✴ Mindfulness can help us turn toward uncomfortable emotions, but it is a practice of self-study, not therapy. For those who have experienced trauma or have mental health concerns, seeking support from a professional counselor is highly encouraged before or in combination with your mindfulness practice.

Nine Attitudes of Mindfulness

(Kabat-Zinn, 1990)

1. Beginner's Mind
2. Non-judging
3. Acceptance/Allowing
4. Letting go
5. Trust
6. Patience
7. Non-striving
8. Gratitude
9. Generosity

To Learn More about Mindfulness and cultivating these attitudes, check out the Earl E. Bakken for Center for Spirituality & Healing offerings https://csh.umn.edu/

Reflection Questions

How do you want to feel today? What creates the conditions for feeling this way?

How might you sit with any difficult emotions that may come up?

Which of the 9 Attitudes of Mindfulness do you already practice? Which ones might you intentionally incorporate?

action

1. the **accomplishment of** a thing, usually over a period of time, in stages, or with the possibility of repetition
2. an **act of will**: behavior, conduct, initiative
3. the **bringing about** of an alteration by force or through a natural agency

origin

from Latin *actionem*
"a putting in motion; a performing, a doing;
public acts, official conduct; lawsuit, legal action"

Day 92:

Inspired action consistent over
time results in growth.
Now that's my kind of equation!

Action:

By practicing mindfulness, we take time to be intentional about how we want to be and what's important to us; we're then better able to focus our attention and align our attitude to take action in meaningful ways rather than being stuck in our automatic thoughts, behaviors, and reactions.

As a Health Coach, I partner with people to support their overall wellbeing. Through conversations, we create space to gain clarity on what's important to them and identify small yet significant steps to move toward meaningful goals.

These small, sustainable action steps taken consistently create intentional behaviors over time. Repeated behaviors become habits that free up your conscious attention. James Clear calls these "Atomic Habits" because they lead to remarkable results (Clear, 2018).

From the Morning Ritual Meditation for Alignment & Flow, Ranjith Vallathol says, "Human beings are creatures of habit. Ninety-five percent of your thoughts and actions today will be a repetition of yesterday."

This is why building in helpful habits today lays the foundation for the future you desire.

Check this out:
Morning Ritual Meditation for Alignment and Flow
https://insig.ht/Ogrxn5oQRub

Reflection Questions

What are you most inspired to do right now?

What does inspired action look like to you?

What helps you sustain action? What kind of support do you need?

"Whatever is good for your soul,
do that."

- Unknown Author

impact

1. the **striking of one body against another**, collision
2. the **effect or impression** of one person or thing on another
3. **to have an effect** or impact

origin

from Latin *impactus*
"to push into, drive into, strike against"

Day 93: Impact

Impact: Becoming more aware and responsible for the effect we have on others and the world around us.

My mom told me to "leave things better than you found them."

Although this was more explicitly taught regarding places and spaces, I realized the implicit message also applied to people, animals, and the wider world.

> I want to live with purpose and make a positive impact each day.
> I want to live in a world where everyone is free to be their full selves and is supported in designing a life aligned with their dreams.

Although I hope I'm meeting these aims, I believe we will never truly know the impact we have on others. The ripple effects of all the tiny moments of our lives will never fully be known.

The best we can do is to put our intentions into aligned action toward the impact we envision. Since we are all human, we will make mistakes along the way. Therefore, it's important to take responsibility for unintended negative impacts we may cause.

Reflection Questions

What do you want your impact to be?

What does that look like? Visualize success.

How will you recognize ripple effects and celebrate successes along the way?

"I've learned that people will forget what you said, people will forget what you did, but people will never forget how you made them feel."

- Dr. Maya Angelou

align - aligns - aligning

1. to **arrange in a line** or to be parallel
2. to adjust to **produce a proper relationship or orientation**
3. **to ally** (oneself, for example) with one side of an argument or cause

origin

from Old French *alignier*
"set, lay in line"

Over the last 5 days I've shared with you 5 elements of mindful awareness: Intention, Attention, Attitude, Action and Impact. The Art of Presence is discovering how these components interact and support one another. This requires being aligned.

Reflection Questions

What helps you stay aligned?

Who are you aligned with?

How does your body tell you when you are out of alignment?

pep

1. **energy and high spirits**; vim
2. to **bring energy or liveliness to,** invigorate

origin

from 1912, shortened form of *pepper* (n.),
"vigor, energy"

Day 95: Pep

I wake up pretty early (5 am) most mornings. I have a lovely morning routine that helps me feel aligned. It includes meditation (10-15 min), journaling or reading (10-15 min), and a workout (20-30 min) then coffee.

Although I'm tired when I wake up, at some point through this ritual, I notice the initial instance of energy. The word that comes to mind at this moment is pep. I feel a pep in my step and excitement for the day ahead.

Having some time to take care of myself first thing in the morning helps me have the energy to care for others and the tasks of the day.

This pep usually takes a bit of a slump around 2:30 pm and generally completely wears off by 8:30 pm, but I'm grateful for practices and people who support me.

Reflection Questions

What gives you a pep in your step?

What does your morning routine consist of? What do you want to add, remove, or continue to support your sustained energy for the day ahead?

What does pep feel like in your body?

compassion

compassion

1. **a deep sympathy for the sorrows of others, with an urge to alleviate their pain**

origin

"feeling of sorrow or deep tenderness for one who is suffering
or experiencing misfortune"
from mid-14c., *compassioun*
literally **"a suffering with another"**

Day 96:

Compassion

Caregivers
Car rides
Coffee
Compassion

Aside from starting with the letter 'c,' what do these things have in common?
They are all part of my morning routine during the school year. Today is the first day of school for our kids. This means a change in routine during this time of transition.

For us, the first week is usually full of excitement, meaning getting ready and out the door is easier. However, as the school year wears on, it can become a challenge. Rushing, yelling, and running late are not great combinations for a good day. This leaves everyone feeling crumby. Even with the best-laid plans and intentions, we are all human, and these days happen more often than we'd like.

When I look at the long line of vehicles in the drop-off line, it can be easy to imagine Hallmark moments filling other parents' mornings, and I can get trapped in comparison. Yet, if I catch that thought, it's also likely that many of those families also had a rough start, and I can extend compassion and well-wishes to them, too.

I often think there should be a radio program from 7:30 - 8:30 am called "Coffee and Compassion," made especially for caregivers who just dropped off their kids after a tough start as a potential reset. I think space at school for kiddos to process would also be ideal.

Did you know?

- ☀ Research shows that being a "good enough" parent is being attuned to your child's emotional needs 30% of the time to raise a securely attached child. (See the attachment research of Ed Tronick, John Bowlby, Mary Ainsworth, and Donald Winnicott).

- ☀ This means that even when we are misaligned 70% of the time, we still can have a strong attachment to our kids.

- ☀ During these times of misalignment, we are showing our children that we are human too and we have a chance to model how to move through challenges.

- ☀ These misalignments are opportunities to repair ruptures in the relationship and navigate challenging emotions and situations. Trust is built through repairing ruptures.

With this in mind, it brings me back to school drop-offs and some quick math:

My oldest is 15 and will be driving next year.

This is the last year I'll be doing school drop-offs. There are 176 days in this school year, which means that if I "get it right" 53 mornings, I'm doing "good enough."

I hope it's more than 53 days, but it leaves space for grace and compassion.

Reflection Questions

What would aiming for "good enough" offer you?

What helps you to repair ruptures in relationships? How might you leave space for grace and compassion?

How might you extend well-wishes (also known as lovingkindness) to others who are going through challenges?

boundaries

boundaries

1. something that indicates a **border or limit**
2. the border or limit so indicated

origin

"that which indicates the **limits of anything**,"
from 1620s, from <u>bound</u> + <u>ary.</u>

Strictly, a visible mark indicating a dividing line, a bound being
the limit or **furthest point of extension of any one thing**.

Day 97: Boundaries

Hedgehogs represent gentleness and boundaries as "they maintain composure, poise, and tranquility in the face of hardship."

In early 2022, I participated in a program focused on Organic Boundaries with Sherene Cauley, founder of The Nurtured Life. Learn more about Sherene's work supporting collective wellbeing at www.thenurturedlife.org

Here is a snapshot of what I learned: Rather than boundaries being firm, unmoving barriers to connection built for self-protection, they are naturally occurring, organic, flexible conduits of connection that are ever-changing and grow around needs.

We must be present with ourselves and the sensations of our bodies and our energy, as well as the energy of others, to notice subtle shifts and openings to honor our own and each other's needs.

It's easy to be unaware, dismiss, or disrespect our own and each other's boundaries based on our culture, which often violates boundaries. This is by design to keep us separate and striving

Reflection Questions

What practices protect your peace and support connection?

What boundaries might you need to support your needs?

How does your body tell you if your boundaries have been disrespected?

Learn more about hedgehog symbolism https://spiritofsapphire.co.uk/hedgehog-symbolism/

recognize

rMg

recognized - recognizing

1. to know to be something that has **been perceived before**
2. **to know or identify** from experience or knowledge
3. to perceive or **show acceptance of the validity or reality of**

origin

from Old French *reconoiss,*
"to know again, identify, recognize"

Day 98: Recognize

Today, the word 'recognize' comes up a few different times, in a few different ways. Have you ever noticed how it only takes a glimpse of seeing someone familiar to know it's them?

Or how when you get what I call 'soul shimmers' (aka, tingles or good goosebumps), is it your body's recognition of something more profound happening? Or having an ah-ah moment when you are inspired by something seemingly new but resonates so deeply that it feels true and familiar. My favorite part of being a health coach is seeing the twinkle in clients' eyes when they get that spark of inspiration from their innate wisdom.

Finally, during this project, I noticed how art touches us and how creativity connects us. Perhaps it's the recognition of the reflection of ourselves in another that reminds us we are real and worthy of belonging.

Reflection Questions

What practices support you in recognizing your own innate wisdom of deeper knowing?

Notice when you get a 'soul shimmer' sensation. What were you doing? These are clues!

What sights do you recognize that bring you right back to your childhood?

future

1. **the indefinite time yet to come**
2. something that will happen in time to come
3. a prospective or expected condition, especially one considered about **growth, advancement, or development**

origin

from Latin *futurus*,
"going to be, yet to be"

Day 99: Future

Near the end of this 100-day project, I wonder what comes next.

I tend to jump right into the next thing or set the next goal without space to soak in the accomplishments and lessons learned—time to pause and ponder.

I'm unsure what the future holds, but I look forward to seeing what unfolds.

Reflecting on this project reminds me that small, consistent actions over time add up. They move dreams into reality through doing, being, and becoming.

Reflection Questions

What helps you sit in the space between the past and future?

What might you do to help your future self (tomorrow, next month, next year)?

What small steps might you take to move a dream into reality?

complete

completing - completed

1. having all parts or elements; **lacking nothing; whole; entire; full**
2. **finished**; ended; concluded
3. thorough; total, undivided, uncompromised, or unqualified

origin

from Latin *completus,*
"to fill up, complete"
transferred to "fulfill, finish (a task)"

Day 100: Complete

And that's a wrap!
✨ 100 days of Aligned Enchantment ✨

I'm not sure what it is yet, but it feels like there are a few more steps to complete this project fully:

- Slow down, let it settle in, glean the wisdom enchantment has shared with me, and continue to create space for creativity.
- Rather than feeling like chasing the next thing, it feels like circling back to close the loop.
- Gathering up the individual pieces, tying up loose ends, and putting a bow on them to make them a complete collection.

Reflection Questions

What helps you stay focused to fully finish what you started?

How do you celebrate milestones and soak in the moments following an accomplishment?

Remind yourself that you are fully creative, capable, and complete. Right now. Just as you are. What do you notice?

Dear Enchantment,

What would you have me know or do today?

Dear One,

Unfurl the tension, unpack your fears, **unload** your worries, and **unplug** from distractions.

Let your **imagination** run **wild**.

Befriend the silly, **squirrelly** part of yourself and **remember** to **play**!
Put some **pep** in your step, wander with **whimsy**, or go **frolic** in a field.

Feel the **bubbly effervesce** of the **sol** shimmers that result when you **decide** to **dabble** in **delight**.

Trust that **flash** of **insight**, follow the **gentle** pull of **intrigue**, or reminisce in a **nostalgic notion**.
Practice **patience** to see what **emerges**.
Allow it to **flow** and refuse to **rush**.

Simplify to **create** space for **serendipity**.
Lean on **luck** and be **open** to the **potential**.
Leap into the unknown **future**.

Let your **heart** be your **compass**.
Harness that **wisdom** to set an **intention rooted** in **love** & collective **care**.
Anchor your **attention** on the **glorious treasure held** within this moment.
Align your **attitude** with **optimistic hope**.
Use this **clarity** to take **inspired action** for **empowered change**.
Glide purposefully but let your mind **drift** and daydream knowing the ripple
effect of your **impact** will never be **complete** but will always **be enough**.

When the weight of the world feels too heavy, **learn** in order to act **locally.**
When there are **no words**, or you feel conflicted or constricted,
Find a **serene** space to **nestle** in, let your thoughts **settle**, and your sorrow be
soothed.
Envelop yourself in **compassion** feeling **snug** and **secure** until you find your
voice and next right step.

Rain or **shine**, **plant** seeds of **kindness**.
Watch the **good grow** and the **beloved bloom** beyond **boundaries**.
Recognize it's within your nature to **nurture** and **behave** in a **bold** and
blissful manner.
Persist with **pride** and **regal confidence** knowing you are kissed by **kismet**.
Be willing to **morph** with the **seasons** and **ease** into **tranquil transitions**.

Love,

Notes & Reflections

Acknowledgments

Special thanks to the support of my family, friends, and these inspiring humans:

Heather Wilde
Wilde, Heather. Hezzie Mae, 2024. https://www.hezziemae.com/

Sarah Seidelmann
Seidelmann, Sarah. Follow Your Feel Good, 2024. https://followyourfeelgood.com

Diane Banigo
Banigo, Diane. Ignited Faces of Beauty (iFOB) LLC. 2024. https://ifobconsult.com

Tiara Cash
Cash, Tiara. Crowned Vitta, LLC. 2024. https://crownedvitta.com/

Jilly Shipway
Shipway, Jilly. Yoga Through the Year. 2015. https://www.yogathroughtheyear.com

Farmer John & Sunshine Kelly
Farm Sol, 2024. www.farmsol.online/

Julie Zaruba Fountaine
Zaruba Fountaine, Julie. Empower Possible, LLC. 2024. https://empowerpossible.com

Sherene Cauley
Cauley, Sherene. The Nurtured Life, 2024. https://www.thenurturedlife.org/

For more information about my work through Art of Presence, please visit:
artofpresence.org
hello@artofpresence.org

Bibliography

Allred, Lisa. "Good Enough Parenting." SAS Institute. 2024. Accessed July 29, 2023. www.blogs.sas.com/content/efs/2020/10/12/good-enough-parenting.

Bashar, Darius. "Creativity is a Relationship." Insight Timer App. Insight Network. Inc. 2021. Accessed July 29, 2023. www.insighttimer.com/dariusbashar/guided-meditations/creativity-is-a-relationship.

Bashar, Darius. "What if it were easy?" Insight Timer App. Insight Network. Inc. 2021. https://insighttimer.com/dariusbashar/guided-meditations/what-if-it-were-easy-morning-meditation

Bowlby, J. A Secure Base: Parent-child Attachment and Healthy Human Development. New York, NY: Basic Books, 1988.

Bowlby, J, Ainsworth, M., Boston, M., & Rosenbluth, D. The effects of mother-child separation: A follow-up study. British Journal of Medical Psychology 29, no. 2 (1956) 11-247.

Blaise, Aaron. Bear Cub Character Bear Art. Shutterstock. 2024. Accessed July 29, 2023. www.paintingvalley.com.

Brach, Tara. "RAIN: A Practice of Radical Compassion." RAIN: Recognize, Allow, Investigate, Nurture. Tara Brach, PhD, 2023. Accessed March 2, 2024. www.tarabrach.com/rain.

Brown, Stuart. "The Practice of Play with Dr. Stuart Brown." Taking of your Wellbeing. Earl E. Bakken Center for Spirituality and Healing, Accessed March 2, 2024. www.takingcharge.csh.umn.edu/practice-play-dr-stuart-brown.

Caramela, Sammi. "Tiber Lily: Meaning and Symbolism of This Beautiful Flower. A-Z Animals. 2008-2024. Accessed July 29, 2023. www.a-z-animals.com/blog/tiger-lily-meaning-and-symbolism.

Carter, Lou. "What Do Rabbits Symbolize? Rabbit Symbolism Meaning" Rabbit Care Tips. 8/11/2021. Accessed July 29, 2023. www.rabbitcaretips.com.

Clear, James. Atomic Habits: An Easy & Proven Way to Build Good Habits & Break Bad Ones. New York, NY, Penguin Audio, an imprint of the Penguin Random House Audio Publishing Group. 2019.

Cohen, Zachary. "What is Collective Effervescence?" The Core Collaborative. 8/30/2021. Accessed July 29, 2023. https://thecorecollaborative.com/what-is-collective-effervescence/

David, Lauren. "Spiritual Symbolism & Meaning Of The Peacock + What To Do If You Keep Seeing Them." Mind Body Green. 3/27/2023. Accessed July 29, 2023. www.mindbodygreen.com.

David, Lauren. "4 Cultural Meanings Of The Dragonfly + Why To Pay Attention To This Critter." Mind Body Green. October 25, 2022. Accessed March 4, 2024. www.mindbodygreen.com.

Evans-Wentz, W. Y. Chauchoma and Sacred Mountains. Stanford: Stanford University Press.1981 https://link.springer.com.

Bibliography (cont'd)

Gilbert, Elizabeth. Big Magic: Creative Living Beyond Fear; Penguin Group USA, 2015.

Hart, Christopher. How to Draw a Bear Cub - Fun & Easy for Beginners. 2015. www.youtube.com/watch?v=yPGlZa5N2FE.

"Hedgehog Symbolism: Understand The Spiritual Meaning And Dream Meaning of Hedgehogs" Spirit of Sapphire. 2024. Accessed 7/29/2023. https://spiritofsapphire.co.uk/hedgehog-symbolism/

Jeffery, Al. "Create a Clearing to Listen In." Insight Timer App.Insight Network. Inc. 2021. https://insig.ht/wYyqon0w9sb.

Johnson, Mariann. Cultivating Mindful Attitudes: A Personal and Relational Practice. Earl E Bakken Center for Spirituality and Healing. 2/1/22. Accessed July 29, 2023. https://csh.umn.edu/news.

Kabat-Zinn, Jon. Full Catastrophe Living: Using the Wisdom of Your Body and Mind to Face Stress, Pain, and Illness. New York: Delta. 1990.

Krisch, Joshua A. "Do elephants really 'never forget'?" LiveScience. Future US, Inc. 1/29/2023. Accessed July 29, 2023. https://www.livescience.com/do-elephants-have-good-memories.

Liesveld, Curt. "Learner - Gallup Theme Thursday Shorts Season 1." CliftonStrengths. 12/12/2014. Accessed 7/29/2023. https://www.youtube.com/watch?v=hQYxyXsuMec

"Live your Best Life Using Your Strengths." Gallup. 2024. Accessed 7/29/2023. https://www.gallup.com/cliftonstrengths/en/home.aspx

Marcus, B., Napolitano, M., King, A., Lewis, B., Whiteley, J., Albrecht, A., Parisi, A., Bock, B., Pinto, B., Sciamanna, C., Jakicic, J., Papandonatos, G. Examination of print and telephone channels for physical activity promotion: Rationale, design, and baseline data from Project STRIDE. Contemporary Clinical Trials, 28. No. 1(2006). 90-104.

"Matrescence: The complex reality of your birth as a mother." Cradlewise, Inc. 2020-2023. Accessed July 29, 2023. https://cradlewise.com/blog/matrescence-your-birth-as-a-mother.

Merriam-Webster. Encyclopaedia Britannica Company. 2024. www.merriam-webster.com.

National Multiple Sclerosis Society. 2024. https://www.nationalmssociety.org.

Norris, Rebecca. "The Symbolic Meaning of Crossing Paths With a Monarch Butterfly." Well+Good. 9/28/2023. www.wellandgood.com/monarch-butterfly-meaning.

Northrup, K. (2025, April/May) Good with Money. [Online workshop]. https://katenorthrup.com.

Online Etymology Dictionary. Douglas Harper. 2021-2024. www.etymonline.com.

"Orange Lilly Meaning: The Truth About it." FloraQueen. 2002-2022. Accessed July 29, 2023. www.floraqueen.com/blog/the-truth-about-the-orange-lily-meaning.

"Our Dragonfly Symbol" Emily Fredricks Foundation. 2024. www.emilyfredricksfoundation.org/about.

Potter, Dave. "Mountain Meditation." Palouse Mindfulness: Mindfulness-Based Stress Reduction 2024. https://palousemindfulness.com/meditations/mountain.html.

Powell, B., Cooper, G., Hoffman, K., & Marvin, R. S. The Circle of Security Intervention: Enhancing Attachment in Early Parent-Child Relationships. New York, NY. The Guilford Press, 2014.

Ryan, R. M., & Deci, E. L. Self-determination theory and the facilitation of intrinsic motivation, social development, and well-being. American Psychologist, 55. No. 1 (2000): 68–78. https://doi.org/10.1037/0003-066X.55.1.68.

Salzberg, Sharon. "What is Loving-Kindness? And how to practice it in an era of intolerance." Medium. 2/28/2018. Accessed July 29, 2023. https://medium.com.

Shapiro, S.L., Carlson, L.E., Astin, J.A., & Freedman, B. "Mechanisms of Mindfulness" Journal of Clinical Psychology, 62. No. 3 (2006): 373-386.

Shipway, Jilly. Chakras for Creativity: Meditations & Yoga-based Practices to Awaken Your Creative Potential; Woodbury, MN: Llewellyn Publication, 2022.

The Free Dictionary.Com. Farlex. 2024. www.thefreedictionary.com.

"The Meaning and Symbolism of the Sunflower." Thursd. 2024. https://thursd.com/articles/meaning-symbolism-sunflower.

Tran, Mia. "Spiritual Benefits of Aloe Vera: How to Use Aloe Vera for the Spiritual Purpose." Natural Scents. 2/25/2024. https://naturalscents.net/spirituality/aloe-vera-spiritual-benefits.

Tronick, Ed & Gold, Claudia. The Power of Discord: Why the ups and Downs of Relationships are the Secret to Building Intimacy, Resilience, and Trust; New York, NY: Little, Brown Spark, 2020.

"What is the Circle of Security?" Circle of Security International, 2022. Accessed July 29, 2023. www.circleofsecurityinternational.com/circle-of-security-model/what-is-the-circle-of-security.

Winnicott, Donald Woods. "Good-enough mother." Oxford Reference.; Accessed March 3, 2024. www.oxfordreference.com.

ABOUT THE AUTHOR

Rachel Gilbertson aims to live with purpose and make a positive impact each day. She has a passion for supporting *whole-person and collective wellbeing*. Her mission is to inspire others to practice the art of presence by aligning intention, attention, attitude, action, and impact through coaching, creativity, and classes.

Rachel loves learning and has earned her undergraduate degree in Community Health Education and completed a Master of Education and a graduate minor in Integrative Therapies and Healing Practices. She is a National Board Certified Health & Wellness Coach, a certified Intrinsic Coach, an A.C.E certified personal trainer, and a mindfulness facilitator.

Rachel wants to live in a world where everyone is free to be their full self and is supported in designing a life aligned with their dreams. Rachel shares her life in Northern Minnesota with her husband, three kids, three dogs, and two cats. They enjoy everything from life's big adventures to finding the extraordinary in the ordinary.

Photography: Sam Gilbertson

Hezzie Mae provides authors with essential services: meticulous *manuscript preparation*, tailored *publishing*, expressive *illustrations* that resonate with emotion, and comprehensive *marketing support*.

Our marketing coaching for authors offers personalized support to authors who want to boost book sales or navigate marketing challenges without heavily relying on social media.

At Hezzie Mae, we are committed to enhancing your writing journey and helping you achieve your publishing goals while staying true to your unique vision and storytelling style.

You are invited to check out Hezzie Mae's latest releases on our website, where we also offer wholesale pricing.

www.HezzieMae.com

Hezzie
Mae
BOOK PUBLISHING

www.ingramcontent.com/pod-product-compliance
Lightning Source LLC
Chambersburg PA
CBHW082144120626
46553CB00010B/2757